Prentice-Hall

America's Role in World Affairs Series

Dankwart A. Rustow, Editor

RUPERT EMERSON
    Africa and United States Policy

WALTER GOLDSTEIN
    Military Strategy in World Politics

WILLIAM E. GRIFFITH
    Cold War and Coexistence: Russia, China, and the United States

ERNST B. HAAS
    The Web of Interdependence: The United States
    and International Organizations

M. DONALD HANCOCK and DANKWART RUSTOW, eds.
    Readings in American Foreign Policy

STANLEY HOFFMANN
    Europe and United States Policy

CHARLES BURTON MARSHALL
    The Burden of Decision: American Foreign Policy Since 1945

JOHN D. MONTGOMERY
    Foreign Aid in International Politics

WILLIAM C. OLSON
    The Making of United States Foreign Policy

DANKWART A. RUSTOW
    The New Setting of World Politics

KALMAN H. SILVERT
    Latin America and United States Policy

WAYNE A. WILCOX
    Asia and United States Policy

America's Role in World Affairs Series

ERNST B. HAAS
University of California, Berkeley

The Web of Interdependence

The United States and International Organizations

PRENTICE-HALL, INC., ENGLEWOOD CLIFFS, N.J.

C-13-947838-8
P-13-947820-5

Library of Congress Catalog Card No.: 69-14549

Current printing (last number):
10 9 8 7 6 5 4 3 2 1

PRENTICE-HALL INTERNATIONAL, INC. *London*
PRENTICE-HALL OF AUSTRALIA, PTY. LTD. *Sydney*
PRENTICE-HALL OF CANADA, LTD. *Toronto*
PRENTICE-HALL OF INDIA PRIVATE LTD. *New Delhi*
PRENTICE-HALL OF JAPAN, INC. *Tokyo*

America's Role in
World Affairs Series

Specialized knowledge and practical experience combine to lay the solid foundations for this survey of AMERICA'S ROLE IN WORLD AFFAIRS. Eleven distinguished authors distill their insights, refined in years spent as responsible government officials, as high-level advisers to governments, in prolonged field research, and in teaching at our leading universities. Their volumes emphasize the lasting realities underlying current conflict, the political forces in the present that will shape the world of the future. Separately, each volume in the series is a concise, authoritative analysis of a problem area of major significance. Taken as a whole, the series gives a broader and more diversified coverage than would be possible in a single book on American foreign policy and international relations.

An introductory volume by the series editor appraises the rapidly changing environment of foreign policy in the second half of the twentieth century—the revolution of modernization, the multiplication of sovereign states, and the tightening network of communication around the globe. In bold and deft strokes, William C. Olson analyzes the forces of public opinion, congressional action, and planning and implementation in the executive branch that combine to shape American foreign policy. Charles Burton Marshall takes the reader to the inner councils of United States policy as he retraces with wit, urbanity, and a lively sense of drama some of the crucial turning points in our foreign relations.

Three volumes deal systematically with some of the major instruments of contemporary foreign policy. Walter Goldstein cogently links the breathless pace of military technology in a nuclear age to some of the perennial dimensions of human conflict and strategic calculation. The wide range of uses—the possibilities and limitations—of foreign aid yield to John D. Montgomery's penetrating treatment. Ernst B. Haas combines sober realism with a passionate sense of human interdependence in his succinct account of the contemporary pattern of international organization.

Another group of volumes takes us to regions where the drama of modern international politics is being enacted. The intimate and yet often frustrating relations between the United States and Western Europe are sharply illuminated by Stanley Hoffmann's irony and subtle understanding. William E. Griffith clarifies the awesome issues of Cold War and coexistence in the triangular relations among the United States, the Soviet Union, and Communist China. Wayne Ayres Wilcox, in a synthesis of rare breadth and depth, allows the reader to grasp the full complexities of that geographic concept called Asia. The problems of new states, with their bitter memories of the colonial past and their ardent hopes for a better future, are presented with sympathy and skepticism in Rupert Emerson's volume on Africa. Kalman H. Silvert draws on two decades of travel and study and on his keen sense for the explosive issues of evolution vs. revolution as he sums up the record of our relations with Latin America.

The contributors have sought no consensus of policy preference and no narrow uniformity of scholarly method. They share a conviction that policy must operate within a context of circumstance that allows now a wider, now a narrower, choice of alternatives and that sound policy must be formulated from a thorough knowledge of that context. They hold that valid theory in the social sciences must rise upon solid empirical foundations. They also believe that clarity and conciseness do not detract from true scholarship but, on the contrary, enhance it. Within such broad assumptions, each author has applied his specialized knowledge and his practical experience to one distinctive facet of AMERICA'S ROLE IN WORLD AFFAIRS.

DANKWART A. RUSTOW

Contents

1

Nations and Statesmen in the International System

As the United Nations stands at approximately the quarter-century mark, many Americans question the value of the network of institutions into which the strands of American policy are woven. Some wish to strengthen and extend the ties, to make American foreign policy almost identical with American participation in international organizations. Others wish to reexamine, reduce, or even eliminate our enmeshment. The debate promises to continue.

American policy has by no means been consistent, steady, and unwavering in international organizations since the founding of the UN in 1945. Institutions, obligations, and responsibilities now accepted have developed gradually in the intervening years. Many were not the result of deliberate choice and planning in 1945. Some were accepted grudgingly by American policy-makers; others are being debated now and have not yet been accepted at all.

As early aims fall short of achievement, governments somehow "learn" to adapt their policies toward, and hopes in, international institutions. How does this learning occur?

INTERNATIONAL INTERDEPENDENCE AND SOCIAL LEARNING

We can conceptualize two different learning processes. One is purely national and thus autonomous of international influences. Political actors may learn from successes and failures at home, their learning being reinforced by demands made upon them by their own citizens. For example, success in dealing with economic crises through a certain method of planning may induce an attitude of international planning predicated on the same principles; failure in stemming a political revolt of an ethnic minority at home may imply a new attitude toward internationally fomented internal war. There is, of course, no guarantee that separate national learning processes in different countries will proceed along similar, symmetrical, or parallel courses; one country's lesson may be the opposite of her neighbor's —as illustrated by the contemporary cases of Cambodia and Thailand.

The other learning process is "systemic"; i.e., the impulse proceeds from an international experience to a national reaction. Experience in international dealings—encounters with the "system" of international relations and institutions—changes the ways in which national policy-makers react, causes them to adapt or to revise their expectations, thus possibly changing the system itself because of a new pattern of demands and response.

Moreover, the lessons taught by social learning differ in terms of their scope and permanence. Short-term forces may effect adaptations in policy. The diplomat perceives a switch in alliance of an important nation; the soldier sees military regimes rising in underdeveloped nations; the technical assistance expert is alert to a drop in the world price of coffee. Such observations are responsible for the majority of policy changes that are visible to us. Long-range impulses are not so readily identifiable; but they are powerful shapers of future attitudes, frustration, hopes, and fears. The rate of technical and scientific innovation, diffusion of ideas and practices, alterations in population ratios, sudden breakthroughs in the mastery of nature —these are long-range trends that are the meat and drink of scholarly observers who warn of future probabilities or advocate massive changes in approach. Statesmen and governments, preoccupied with short-range change, are too often taken by surprise when confronted with the new environmental forces labeled the "multifold trend" by Herman Kahn. The network of short- and long-range forces, the constraints and institutions devised to channel them, and the immersion of the national interest of the United States in this pattern make up the web of interdependence.

Henry Kissinger provides us with a half-real and half-hypothetical demonstration of national and systemic learning processes at work: in the years since 1945, the number of independent states has multiplied, the scope of national power has become more diffuse, the reach of ideas has grown downward into previously inert layers of all societies, communication across and within nations has become instantaneous, and ideologies have become universal. In short, everybody influences everybody else all the time. This much is clearly seen by the observer and reflects long-run forces. But it is only dimly and intermittently recognized in the perceptions and policies of political actors.

Short-run political action is determined by three styles of leadership, each typical of a particular kind of national society active in the post-1945 international scene. The styles breed mutual distrust. The most familiar style is the bureaucratic-pragmatic mode of leadership familiar to the West, stressing practical aims, the rational choice of means, quiet consultation, and negotiation. Almost equally familiar is the more ideological style of

Communist nations, with its claim to an objective "science of society" which gives them a "certain" purchase on social reality, contrasting sharply with the skewed vision of reality attributed by Communist actors to their "bourgeois" counterparts. Finally, there is also a charismatic-revolutionary style typical of many new nations, as exemplified by a Castro or a Sukarno. Such leadership is interested in a vision of the future that is purely political—everything else is instrumental toward the "political kingdom" of which Nkrumah always spoke. The state must hold together a fragmented society and hence must be authoritarian. Its leadership then seeks to solve intractable domestic problems by using foreign policy more extensively than Western and Communist leadership uses it.

Consequently, in the short run, the activities of the international system will stress conflict, because these three types of actors find it impossible to negotiate meaningfully. They cannot agree on the definition of an issue, on what constitutes a reasonable proposal. Each depends heavily on immediate success as measured by domestic repercussions, on the short-term goal of immediate survival.

Thus far in our argument, a domestic setting has induced a type of "learning" that conditions the actor to distrust his opposite number in the international system. But what if the process of encountering his opposite number year after year, with constantly mounting dangers *perceived equally by all,* induces him to abandon some aspect of his previous stance? What if a shared sense of danger develops and begets a more trusting pattern of response? Were that to happen, systemic learning would be at work. There is some evidence that this has indeed happened in the United Nations and elsewhere in recent years.

Our central problem is the position of the United States in a web of interdependence. Do its leaders perceive the United Nations as facilitating or decreasing American global influence? Has that perception changed since the birth of our contemporary organizations in the years immediately following World War II? If so, has the change in perception been due to domestic or systemic learning? If learning was systemic, have United States' attitudes and policy been adapted to reflect the long-range independent change factors we noted above? If so, what does that suggest about the "rules" and "constraints" of a future international system?

That both scholars and actors, writing fifteen or twenty years after the birth of the UN, see new American perceptions is not difficult to prove. In 1945 most Americans thought of the UN Charter and institutions as devices to make the world safe for basically peaceful, satisfied, and progressive—if not entirely democratic—nations: the UN Charter implied the American Way of Life writ large. By 1960 there was a widespread recognition that "we cannot value the United Nations, in general terms, as a pro-Western agency and expect the Soviet Union to value it, at our occasional convenience, as an impartial agency of the international community."[1] "We should recognize that there will be times, many times, when the interests of the United Nations, an organization devoted more and more to the needs

[1] Inis L. Claude in Francis O. Wilcox and H. Field Haviland, eds., *The United States and the United Nations* (Baltimore: Johns Hopkins, 1961), p. 124.

and wishes of the small states, will not be identical with ours." [2] "The price of participating in any political institution is that you cannot get your way all of the time. . . . The central question is whether the credits exceed the debits, whether as a whole the institution is making a net contribution to the national interest." [3] "And the notion persists that agreement or disagreement among nations at any given time is total—that you cannot hold opposing views on subject A and simultaneously cooperate on subject B. This, of course, is nonsense. . . ." [4] The long-run trends spotted by observers seem clearly to have been recognized by actors. Apparently the United States did learn the rules of a new system as a result of lessons taught *by the system itself.*

Our question now is: what choices are open to the United States as a national entity with changing demands and expectations in the international arena? The point of departure for giving an answer must be the vision of the past, present, and future international systems, long-range views rising above the maelstrom of immediate events and crises, those that have already passed and the ones yet to come. In other words, choices are limited by the international constellation of trends, influences, and forces we label the "system." Why cannot the United States simply cut loose from these influences and, by a supreme act of will, dictate its terms to the world? It can—but it won't. As long as actors seek to maximize gains and minimize losses, they will avoid dramatic moves. And they are therefore the prisoners of history. The logic of compromise and adjustment, as mediated through the way actors perceive their interests, will predispose the United States toward a continuing learning process.

The policy-maker is then free to learn in several ways without making the gesture of supreme defiance, which would be to say, "I shall act as if no constraints were imposed on me and do what I think right. . . ." The United States can recognize basic new forces and influences and can oppose their coming to fruition. It is able to adopt a stance of seeking to freeze international *status quo,* which would be an attempt to *break the web of interdependence.* Alternatively, policy-makers can neglect close attention to long-range trends and can continue along the lines of crisis-by-crisis international accommodation. If they follow this road, they are likely to *strengthen the web,* because the accommodations will imply more complex and more numerous institutional and financial ties with other countries and organizations. Finally, the United States is able to recognize the implications of basic change and identify those that are desirable. It can then respond by weakening its participation in some international activity while strengthening it in others. This response would be to *confuse the web* of interdependence. One aim of this book is to discuss whether the United States will strengthen, break, or confuse the web.

Our first step must be a description of the web over the last fifty years as it appears to the observer. Successive international systems must be

---

[2] Joseph E. Johnson in Wilcox and Haviland, *ibid.,* p. 7.

[3] Richard Gardner, *In Pursuit of World Order* (New York: Praeger, 1964), pp. 119-20.

[4] Harlan Cleveland, "The Capacities of the United Nations," in Wilcox and Haviland, *The United States and the United Nations,* p. ix.

sketched. But we must understand that these systems are not the figment of the observer's imagination but the *resultants* of short-range views and policies adopted by successive actors—as interpreted by the observer. Nations and their statesmen provided the decisions that shaped the events that produced the successive patterns that the observer sketches as systems.

Next, the character of the United States as a collective actor on the world scene will be thrown into relief, compelling us to show that American participation in the web is related to the military, Congress, the Executive, pressure groups, public opinion, and all other institutions and forces of a pluralistic democracy. In this demonstration, we shall treat the hallowed topic of power with some measure of disrespect. Power is the special form of political influence that involves the threat of coercive sanction by one party against another. Influence, more generally, is the ability of one party to get another to do something that the second would not otherwise do. Since we usually have no certain way of knowing the extent to which the second party was unwilling, initially, to do the first's bidding, we cannot speak with any precision about the amount or scope of American world influence. Evaluation is even less precise, as the means of persuasion available to American policy-makers vary from issue to issue. Nor are we in any clearer position regarding power, the ability to exercise influence by threat of punishment. Normally it is assumed that the militarily and industrially stronger nation has more power than the weaker nation and can threaten sanctions accordingly. But the real question is: *will the stronger readily use this power?* Britain in Rhodesia, the Soviet Union in Rumania, and the United States in Cuba all suggest that the answer must be "not necessarily." The *capability* of a nation to coerce should never be confused with the *will* to do so. Will depends on the perception of actors, on their ability to learn the character of constraints. We can discuss changing perceptions without complicating our analysis with the elusive notion of power.

Placing the United States into a global systemic picture, we can determine how American groups and policy-makers formulate specific policy demands in international organizations. The issue areas of concern to us include the following: maintenance of collective security by the United Nations; regional defensive alliances; disarmament and arms control; economic development and technical assistance; world trade and finance; the protection of human rights; decolonization; science, technology, and international planning. We are here concerned with how the actors see issue areas in various periods of time. Have demands changed over time? Have the actors learned to tone down certain demands and voice others? Have policies associated with new demands brought forth results intended by the actors? If so, with what consequences for American satisfaction or dissatisfaction? Have these policies, on the other hand, resulted in unintended and unforeseen results? If so, with what consequences for the degree of American contentment with the web of interdependence? We suspect that the web can be broken, confused, or strengthened largely because unintended results occur far more commonly than expected ones. But we also suspect that the strands owe their strength more to the actors' inability to see beyond the short range, than to their commitment to the glory and virtue of the web.

International organizations appeared on the stage of history with some force and effect in 1919. The total network of international relations since that time—the strands of the web that pass through the League of Nations, the International Labor Organization (ILO), the United Nations, the World Health Organization (WHO), and many others—can be divided into seven "systems."

What is a system? It is a period in the history of international relations during which the crucial characteristics of the web of interdependence differed in some specifiable way from earlier and later characteristics. The characteristics we must observe are: (1) the number of actors and their internal attributes, (2) the international distribution of actor capabilities, (3) the goals that actors pursue, the methods they adopt, and (4) the outcomes of their conflicting goals and methods which they impose on the common structures they have set up; i.e., the "tasks" assigned to international organizations.

MODERN INTERNATIONAL SYSTEMS: TYPES
OF ACTORS AND THEIR CAPABILITIES

We shall confine the notion of "actor" to states that appear as members of universal international organizations: the League of Nations and the United Nations. Occasionally, as with modern China, we also consider as "actors" important states that have not joined such organizations but still influence their decisions. The number of actors grew from about 50 in the early life of the League to the present 125 in the UN. But the character of the member states changed even more dramatically and frequently. We are concerned with the types of regimes that have appeared, because we have reason to believe that there is some relationship between the actors' learning ability and their political characteristics.

Regimes vary in the degree of domestic coercion on which they rest; they differ also in terms of the size and the stability of the ruling elite. Two major kinds of regimes—reconciliation and mobilization polities—are similar in encouraging spontaneous or manipulated political participation of their populations. People are "mobilized" socially and economically; they perceive the relevance of international forces and events. They have demands and opinions—spontaneous or indoctrinated—regarding national and international policy. Moreover, the ruling elites are recruited from the population at large. Social mobility into the elite is fairly common. Reconciliation polities feature discussion, negotiation among claimants for benefits, elections, consensual politics, and limited instrumental policy measures. Mobilization polities feature coercion, full-time manipulation of groups, a cohesive ruling elite (though popularly recruited), and an official ideology that spells out the domestic and international mission of the nation in prophetic and passionate terms, and a devotion to revolutionary policies.

Rigid class distinction and nonparticipation for the bulk of the population are characteristic of modernizing autocracies, traditional and modernizing oligarchies. A traditional oligarchy is a regime composed of a few leading families that monopolize positions of influence in agricultural ownership, church, army, and the professions, while the great bulk of the population is rural and disinterested in politics. Modernizing oligarchies seek to alter this condition by gradually forcing the rural population to enter the national stream of life by way of development projects and political organization; their leaders are usually recruited from professionally oriented and educated descendants of the traditional oligarchs, most often lawyers and army officers. In modernizing autocracies, the traditional ruler himself takes the initiative in modernizing the country, in making a nation of alert and participating individuals. But while he does so, the traditional elite is pressed into service, and class distinctions remain crucial.

Today, a common hybrid called authoritarian polity is committed to gradual and controlled socioeconomic modernization. It is willing—eventually—to allow freedom for all shades of opinion, but it is also concerned with keeping freedom under control while modernization continues. The government is headed by a more or less astute and benign dictator, and he relies on a single party which is actually an uneasy coalition of all regime-oriented elite groups. Popular access into this elite is possible but difficult. Policy tends to be cautious, adaptive, instrumental, and desirous of avoiding messianic ideology. Overt dissent is not tolerated, but private criticism is reflected in the ruling elite.

These types of regimes represent varying degrees of tolerance, democracy, messianic drive, and commitment to revolution; but they also correspond to different levels of technological, economic, and social development. Hence, their number and distribution can materially affect the kinds of demands put forward in international politics and the fervor with which the demands are made. Moreover, the types of adjustments that actors at the receiving end of the demands are compelled to make also depend heavily on the distribution of these characteristics. The presence of an appreciable percentage of oligarchies and authoritarian polities tends to create a world system free from large-scale ideological and physical conflict, because these regimes are not capable of—or interested in—self-assertion, except in a very localized crisis. Mobilization polities, when present in large numbers, tend to have the opposite effect, because of their commitment to charismatic or ideological views and leadership.

Actors differ in their ability to influence one another's behavior. Apart from the will to exercise influence, each nation is endowed with military capability—conventional, nuclear, or both—industrial and scientific capacity, and the ability to launch effective ideological, propagandistic, and subversive offensives. In a period characterized by symmetry, all kinds of capability are distributed so that two actors or two blocs share them about evenly. In a period of heterosymmetry, some third force possesses the kinds of power that *reduce* the aggregate ability of the major blocs to maneuver freely, in *equal proportions*, on the international stage. And in a period characterized by asymmetrical distribution of capability, the third force or forces reduce in *unequal proportions* the capability of the major centers.

Further, we must specify how the distribution of these kinds of capability is clustered around poles or into blocs. When single states "lead" or "dominate" large segments of the globe (through alliances or otherwise), we speak of a polar distribution: bipolar from 1947 until 1955, tripolar in the immediate aftermath of the Bandung Conference, and multipolar since the mass admission of African nations. Note that this multipolarity implied the introduction of a heterogeneous distribution of capability *even though* the third pole possessed neither the nuclear nor the conventional military power to cut into the slices possessed by the United States and the Soviet Union. Symmetry was destroyed because of the ideological-subversive capability of the third bloc and because of its ability to make claims on the economic-industrial capacity of the large nations. The third bloc, however, was led by a changing group of nonaligned nations—India, Egypt, and Yugoslavia—rather than by a single bloc leader. With the decline in the ability of single states to "lead" alliances, we now speak of "multibloc" clusterings of power in preference to "poles."

The changing distribution of capability and the growing proportional share of all types of nations other than traditional oligarchies and reconciliation polities are apparent from Table 1. These two sets of characteristics taken together set the scene for the action nations impose on the web of interdependence.

AIMS AND METHODS OF ACTORS

The objectives of national foreign policy have always been classified as *revisionist* or *status quo* oriented. States wish either to keep things as they are or to work for a change favoring their goals. What are the major substantive issues of modern international relations that cause states to behave as *status quo* or revisionist powers?

The legitimacy of existing political boundaries is one such issue. States demanding territorial adjustments, cessions of provinces, the removal of colonial administrations, and tribal reunifications are revisionists; governments taking their stand on the legitimacy of existing borders—a position usually cloaked in the phrase "respect for international obligations and treaties"—are not. The expansion of a specific ideology, whether by conquest or propaganda linked with externally-supported subversion, is another aspect of the same larger issue. Another issue is international economics. Should there be a "natural" division of labor between raw material producers and industrial countries? Should there be a concerted effort to make everybody industrialize? Is the most-favored-nation clause an instrument of economic oppression or a device to assure equality? A revisionist state aims at the reduction of the superiority of the industrialized West; the West itself has taken a *status quo* position much of the time. The universal protection of human rights, through international legal obligations and possibly intervention, is another issue area. Revisionists stress such a role; *status quo* powers emphasize the domestic character of such questions. One may quibble over whether the disarmament and arms control question is a subaspect of the territorial and ideological security issue or whether it should be considered as an issue in its own right. Revisionists stress the danger of arms—the arms of other powers—while *status quo* powers emphasize the need for caution and the demands of security. Finally, the promises and dangers of science and its relationship to social change have emerged as an

TABLE 1 · INTERNATIONAL SETTINGS, 1919-1968
Members of League of Nations or UN

Period and number of members	Polities (per cent of total membership)						Capability distribution
	Rec.	Mob.	M.A.	T.O.	M.O.	Auth.	
1919-31 League: 55 (1925)	51	2	5	35	2	5	Unipolar victor group; isolated dissenters
1932-40 League: 57 (1935)	33	7	10	37	2	10	Bipolar asymmetrical
1945-47 UN: 53 (1946)	43	11	6	34	4	2	Unipolar victor group
1948-51 UN: 60 (1950)	50	13	5	25	5	2	Tight bipolar symmetrical
1952-55 UN: 61 (1953)	46	13	7	19	8	7	Loose bipolar heterosymmetrical
1956-60 UN: 82 (1958)	43	19	15	10	6	7	Tripolar heterosymmetrical
Since 1961 UN: 116 (1965)*	41	19	13	6	8	9	Multipolar heterosymmetrical

* Includes six African states which were not classified for lack of data. UN membership figures (and the percentage for mobilization systems) do not include Ukraine and Byelorussia.

Rec.—Reconciliation polity   T.O.—Traditional oligarchy
Mob.—Mobilization polity   M.O.—Modernizing oligarchy
M.A.—Modernizing autocracy   Auth.—Authoritarian polity

international issue area; *status quo* countries tend to defend the promises of science and the need for unfettered diffusion of techniques and ideas while the revisionists are more alert to implicit dangers. Note, however, that on this issue the developed countries are those who act as revisionists.

The types of methods available to nations in reaching their goals do not change very rapidly. What matters to us is which methods are predominant in any one historical system. Means have included the marshaling of national armaments (both nuclear and conventional), strategic planning and counterplanning, resulting in the eventual institutionalization of the nuclear balance of terror. Mutual thermonuclear deterrence thus came to be the major method relied upon by the superpowers. Conventional capability for fighting local or limited wars has been cultivated by almost a. nations, large and small. In the inevitable confrontations that have ensued, the dominant methods have been alliance-building, threat, and appeasement. In the realm of ideological technique we have seen the flowering of systematic propaganda, large-scale "international information" programs designed to praise the home state and to defame the opponent, the encouragement of dissident movements in the opponent's territory, and the support of subversive activity. In the field of economics, the methods have included bilateral and multilateral technical assistance, international lending, emergency relief, and the granting of long-range development funds. Human rights have been extolled, by and large, as a way to hurt the opponent's image and to cater to the ideological commitments of third blocs. Disarmament negotiations have been featured to eliminate threats perceived symmetrically by all parties as well as to score propaganda points. Large-scale scientific conferences and much technical work by international agencies, including international inspection of scientific installations, have been the way of dealing with the issue area of science.

TASKS OF INTERNATIONAL ORGANIZATIONS

The number and character of the nations in each period, when combined with the distribution of capability to influence each other, set the scene for international interaction; their objectives and the methods at their disposal determine the interaction itself.

Thus collective security is an ingredient of each historical system. But it is vital to know whether decisions to use UN force rest on a big power consensus, on bargaining with third forces, or on overwhelming majority support. Are there bargains that involve other issue areas? In shaping collective security policy, how important are collective economic decisions favoring the revisionists? Must human rights be protected in the process? Do third forces extract disarmament or national self-determination concessions in voting for a United Nations police force? In other words, we wish to know whether decisions on any one ingredient overlap with the other issue areas. If so, a widening of the scope of bargaining, discussion, and international activity takes place; if not, the maintenance of collective security is an autonomous task perhaps unrelated to the growth or decline of United Nations influence.

We expect, of course, that the web of interdependence enmeshing the United States and other countries will be stronger to the extent that issues do overlap in the bargaining process, whereas the autonomy of each issue and each partial task will continue to give each member nation a great deal of freedom of national initiative outside the web.

As the actors make clashing demands, negotiate compromises, and strike bargains, the organization is presented with successive tasks involving different combinations of ingredients. During any one period, the types and capabilities of member states result in a network of aims that, in turn, limits the methods appropriate for use by the actors. Table 2 summarizes the aims and methods and describes the resulting bundle that was the task of each period.

Clearly, governments and elites must have "learned" something at crucial points, to make possible the formulation of new aims and the evolution of new tasks. Yet, evidence shows that American elite attitudes and expectations have remained remarkably stable in their view of American participation in the UN as a flexible instrument for anti-Communist world strategy. Perhaps it is the flexibility that has also permitted redefinition of aims, as a result of disappointment in international organizations. In explaining *how* systems change, *how* actors learn to contribute and adapt to international system change, we must first explain how actors perceive domestic and international challenges. Otherwise we will not be able to demonstrate why Americans today advocate more arms control, give more multilateral aid, are more indifferent to the decline of NATO and the OAS, and are more concerned with strengthening UN peacekeeping than they were in 1951 or in 1958.

SYSTEMS, LEARNING, AND PERCEPTION

States "learn," not according to stimulus-response theory, but by adapting their objectives and methods to what can be conceived as attainable by their decision-makers. Learning is a rational process of redefining objectives and changing methods—though the original objectives may ultimately be traced back to "irrational" causes—as leaders discover that persistence with the initial aims is self-defeating or too costly. Hence international bargaining serves as a school in which such lessons are learned.

Considered from the vantage point of the international system itself, this "feedback" model can be summarized differently. The initial objectives of states, as determined by their internal characteristics, are the explicit purposes that lead to demands made of other states in international organizations. In order to gain acceptance of these purposes, a price has to be paid to the purposes of other states, perhaps in a different issue area. The purpose, once accepted by the organization, becomes its immediate task, and its program is built around it. Programs, however, cannot be fully realized, because of faulty planning, inadequate power, low budgets, or national opposition. Disappointment and the hope for better performance in the future is a consequence unintended by those who first framed the task. The lessons of what could and could not be achieved are "fed back" into the national states. They propose new purposes. These can either increase or decrease the task of the organization. In either event, learning has taken place through the feedback process triggered by unintended consequences.

This model of international system transformation credits the international organization with the capacity to produce feedbacks that change the national actors' perceptions. The alternative model we posited puts the emphasis on autonomous changes within nations. In the various domestic sectors—social, economic, and political—developments are conceived as

TABLE 2 · AIMS, METHODS AND TASKS IN INTERNATIONAL SYSTEMS, 1919-1968

Period	Aims of states	Methods of states	Tasks of international organizations
1919-1931	Victors: preservation of political *status quo*, colonial system, global free enterprise. Dissenters: territorial revisionism.	Alliances, arms reduction, improvement of collective security against occasional protest from dissenters.	Achieve collective security based on a Big Power consensus to preserve victors' peace settlement of 1919; give short-term financial aid and emergency relief to victims of World War I; promote arms reduction; preserve free trade and freedom for private financial transactions.
1932-1940	Victors: preservation of entire *status quo*. Dissenters: territorial enlargement, autarky.	Victors: appeasement, slight rearmament. Dissenters: subversion, propaganda, aggression.	None of importance to world politics and economics.
1945-1947	Victors: preservation of new political *status quo*, colonial system, global free enterprise. Dissenters: not heard.	Development of collective security through Big Power consensus; indoctrination and reform of vanquished states; return to competitive world trade and investment.	Achieve collective security through Big Power concert; give emergency relief to victims of World War II; promote world trade rules stressing nondiscrimination and unfettered investment; promote arms reduction.
1948-1951	West: preservation of total *status quo*. East: expansion into Europe and Asia; support of nationalist and communist revolts.	Alliances, bilateral economic aid, multilateral technical aid, propaganda, collective security *against* East, limited war. Subversion, aggression, propaganda, limited war, alliances.	Achieve collective security through authority delegated to U.S. and its allies; give technical assistance; do some regional economic planning for industrialization; advocate Western-controlled human rights.

1952–1955	West: preservation of territorial *status quo*; catering to third forces otherwise.	Alliances, bilateral military and economic aid, nuclear buildup, propaganda.	Achieve collective security through third-world mediation between East and West; give more technical assistance; advocate more general human rights; provide more varied technical services for underdeveloped countries.
	East: aid to nationalist and communist revolts.	Propaganda, subversion, nuclear buildup, alliances.	
	Others: profit from Cold War, for further national and economic development.	Agitation, revolts, economic planning.	
1956–1960	West: adaptation to third force by winning or neutralizing it.	Stabilization of balance of terror; multilateral economic aid; UN stabilization of third force.	Achieve collective security through cautious supranational leadership of UN Secretary-General; give much more extensive economic aid; institute ambitious technical aid programs; intervene collectively for decolonization and human rights.
	East: adaptation to third force by winning or neutralizing it; support for decolonization.	Stabilization of balance of terror; bilateral military and economic aid to new nations; some support for UN aid programs, limited war; propaganda in new states.	
	Others: profit from Cold War for further national and economic development; containment of Cold War and nuclear arms; dislodgment of colonial powers.	Aggression, limited war, more external military and economic aid; legitimation of total national self-determination.	
Since 1961	West: same as above, with Europe more eager than U.S. to adapt; mute Cold War.	Stabilize balance of terror; arms control, decolonization, supranational economic aid; encouragement of trade; less stress on alliances, military aid, propaganda.	Achieve collective security through supranational leadership and Big Power concert; massively promote human rights and decolonization; establish new world trade norms; control arms; explore implications of science; greatly expand investment aid to developing countries.
	East: same as above, with USSR most eager to adapt; mute Cold War; reduction of involvement in new countries while stress is laid on decolonization.	Balance of terror; arms control; encouragement of trade; economic aid; less stress on alliances, military aid, propaganda (*after* nuclear bid in Cuba).	
	Others: same as above (with several different blocs of unaligned states); reorganization of world trade and finance systems.	Subversion, limited war, aggression, regional economic bloc formation.	

proceeding more rapidly and decisively than the learning of lessons fed back from the international system. New demands will then be put on the system, also. These will encounter still other new or opposing demands. The system may not gain any net power at the expense of the member nations but will be transformed, just the same, because it is given new tasks.

System transformation may be due to either or both processes, but only the "feedback" model gives rise to tighter interdependence. The "autonomous internal change" model—in isolation—results in a system that remains largely static. When feedbacks result in adaptive learning among elites, the result is likely to be a stronger system with more autonomous power. But when new tasks evolve from rapidly changing domestic impulses, the system's powers have barely a chance to keep up with the changing mixture of demands. In the actual history of the United Nations and the specialized agencies, the autonomous internal change model comes closer to describing the truth.

But what if actors were to say: We defy the international system to influence our national way of life; we have no demands of the international system except to be left alone? Mao's China and Sukarno's Indonesia suggest that the attempt at full withdrawal from international life may still appear as desirable and feasible to statesmen. The reaction of statesmen and peoples to external and internal demands and lessons is not simply a function of the intensity of the stimulus. The frame of mind, the values, the doctrines and institutions of each nation seem to be important in determining whether the feedback model, the autonomous internal change model, or outright isolationism provides the mechanism for strengthening or breaking the web of interdependence.

Have Americans "learned" to respond primarily to systemic impulses and to adjust to the web so that they reinforce it? There is some evidence that they have. When asked in 1965 whether international or domestic problems facing the United States were most important, 58 per cent stressed international problems. A maximum of 11 per cent, since 1950, thought that the United States should leave the UN. In 1963, 82 per cent felt that the United States must work with other nations. And only 31 per cent felt in 1966 that the United States should withdraw from the UN if Communist China were admitted to the organization.

2

American Democracy and
the International System

DEMOCRACY AND FOREIGN POLICY: THREE MODELS

Whether we look at the phenomenon of American foreign policy-making from the perspective of the actor or the observer, there is no un-ambiguous and universally accepted view on the exact relationship among public opinion, political parties, the State Department, the President, Congress, and the United Nations. We think we know the general thrust of influence, but our intuitive knowledge soon evaporates under the heat of some searching questions. Yet we must know, so that we may discover how, if at all, America adapts to changes in the international system.

In a general way, we all agree that in a democracy, public opinion significantly influences policy. Or are we merely saying that it *should* influence policy, but that actually it may fail to do so? We also agree that public opinion is the sum of individual opinions. These, in turn, are the attitudes we, as citizens, hold toward the role the United States should (or does?) play with respect to other countries. Our attitudes, in turn, are said to be determined by our personalities, but they are also shaped by the values we have imbibed. Are individual attitudes crucial in shaping generalized public opinion? The experts disagree. But they confirm that attitudes are brought to bear on policy-making only in the mold of some specific "situation," such as a crisis or an election, which focuses the attention of the citizen on a choice to be made.

Attitudes and public opinion, it is agreed, do not influence government in a direct way. What intervenes? Certain special groupings of citizens—

interest groups, community groups, respected commentators ("opinion leaders")—speak to and for the individual citizen. Especially influential groups of citizens—elites—are admitted to exist even in democracies, and somehow they intervene between the public and government. But how and when?

Policy is clearly "made" in Washington. Congress discusses policy and votes funds; political parties, in and out of Congress, channel divergent policy demands; officials in government agencies study the needs and position of the United States and make proposals for action; and the President selects from these proposals the course of action he then puts before Congress, the public, and the world. Is he influenced by public opinion, by the parties, by elites? At least three different views exist on *how* public opinion, elite groups, and government are interconnected.

One such model we may call "pure democracy." Individuals are expected to be interested in public issues and the role of America abroad. They are also expected to inform themselves by reading, discussion, and attention to information and interpretations provided by the communication media. United in their local world affairs council, they express their opinions in their votes for congressional and presidential candidates and in the letters they write to their elected representatives. The policy proposed by the President or Congress, then, reflects the sum of informed opinion thrust upward and the balance of informed views. When the American representative in the UN speaks in the name of the United States, he truly speaks for the American people.

What is wrong with this model? Forty per cent of Americans never bother to vote; not less than 75 per cent are ill-informed, emotional in reaction to public affairs, disinterested in foreign policy. Only the more spectacular crises or situations—major wars or space exploits—manage to excite as many as 75 per cent of Americans to a shallow and temporary interest in world affairs. Occasionally, a dramatic crisis suddenly makes the general public wake up. The people may then impulsively embrace a total solution and call for drastic foreign action, or they may break up into several passionate camps, each advocating contradictory total solutions. Perhaps 3 per cent of Americans think about foreign affairs in a way that meets the minimal criteria of rational action: make sure that an individual's attitudes are internally consistent and bear a good correspondence to objectively determined facts. Probably less than 1 per cent combine rational attitudes with a willingness to lobby and influence the government.[1]

In each community there are of course people who combine information, interest, influence, and the willingness to act—the active membership of world affairs councils, committees, and centers. Do they speak for public

---

[1] For these and similar statistics, see Alfred O. Hero, *Americans in World Affairs* (Boston: World Peace Foundation, 1959); James N. Rosenau, *Public Opinion and Foreign Policy* (New York: Random House, 1961). For the period 1945-1955, the most comprehensive treatment of public opinion toward the UN was made by William A. Scott and Stephen B. Withey, *The United States and the United Nations* (New York: Manhattan Publishing Co., 1958). For the period 1955-1966 a complete review is provided by Alfred O. Hero, "The American Public and the UN, 1954-1966," *Journal of Conflict Resolution* (December, 1966). My treatment is a summary of both studies.

opinion? Studies of foreign policy decision-making suggest that such community and opinion leaders often act as *downward* transmission belts of information, attitudes, and policy desires that originate in government. The opinion-transmission process frequently starts at the top and utilizes local opinion leaders to persuade the public, rather than taking the reverse route.

Even then there is no consistent and reliable link between public opinion and congressional or presidential action. For example, Congress voted military aid to Greece, passed the Marshall Plan, and approved U.S. membership in several technical international organizations, even though public opinion polls showed initial majority opposition to these steps. The President acquiesced in the UN's intervening in internal Congolese affairs even though the majority of opinion-makers in the media disapproved of this step. "Democracy is like nearly everything else we do; it is a form of collaboration of ignorant people and experts. . . . The power of the people in a democracy depends on the *importance* of the decisions made by the electorate, not on the *number* of decisions they make." [2] In foreign affairs, at least, the number is too small and the importance too questionable to support the "pure democracy" model.

Hence, why not stress the role of elites intervening between public and government? This brings us to the "pluralist" model. The public is admitted to be as inert as it seems to be. Government then is held to be influenced by myriad organized groups—economic, religious, ethnic, military, professional. Each group defends its own viewpoint on policy, as articulated through the values explicitly shared by the membership, through the ideology professed by each group. Economic, professional, and communication elites at the apex of each group enjoy the support of the mass membership and access to the government—these elites are the brokers between the public and Washington. Democracy is maintained because each coalition of groups is held to bring into being an opposing coalition with which the first has to bargain before policy is made. Public policy, then, is the product of countervailing power wielded by interest groups through their elites.

One possible objection to this model is the undeniable fact that interest and commitment with respect to foreign affairs are consistently and highly correlated with advanced education and high socioeconomic status, irrespective of occupation or group affiliation. It is the educated and highly placed in their respective communities who lead opinion and profess concern for world affairs. Yet it is also true that the same people sometimes hold elite positions in interest groups and may thus meet the demands of the model. A stronger objection is the role claimed for interest groups. Do they really persuade a determined President or a committed majority in Congress? Do all interest groups figure in this process? If not, which ones, how often? Do they really match power with power, coalition with opposing coalition, or does the advice of the expert—the military or civilian bureaucrat in the Pentagon and State Department—count more heavily than the weight of group pressure? When public opinion polls uniformly tell us that in grave international crises, confidence in the President always rises

[2] E. E. Schattschneider, *The Semisovereign People* (New York: Holt, 1960), pp. 137, 140.

—regardless of who occupies the office or the locale of the crisis—we may wonder what happened to countervailing power. To many partisans of the peace movement in the United States the pluralist model appears merely as a façade behind which the "Establishment" rules without check by any opposing force of opinion.

Undeniably, there has usually been a strong American consensus cutting across groups and regions. This fact has led dissenters from this consensus to advance a third model of American democracy, the "power elite" model. It argues that foreign policy decisions are made by an inner clique of industrialists and military men unable and unwilling to depart from a rigid commitment to the economic, racial, and ideological *status quo* —nationally and internationally. Congress, the bureaucracy, and the President are merely the creatures of this Establishment. International peace demands that the power elite be checked and defeated by the masses who are not committed to the *status quo* and who must make themselves into a true countervailing power in order to penetrate and reform the Establishment.

If the argument of the power elite school sounds like the complaint of the groups that have failed to make themselves prevail within American democracy the complaint nevertheless points up some weak spots in the pluralist model. The model is correct in pinpointing the role of interest groups and opposing elites, but it errs in exaggerating the degree of opposition. It is right in minimizing the influence of individuals and of public opinion on foreign policy; it goes too far by ignoring the mood of the public altogether. Pluralism accurately reflects the practice of American democracy in stressing the influence of interest groups on government; it distorts reality by depriving the government of the undeniable capacity to manipulate groups and to ignore them. Between the decision-makers in Washington and the public throughout America there intervene groups and institutions that "make" and "submit" opinions. The opinion-makers are the communication media and the leaders of groups. At the same time, the leaders of interest groups also submit opinions to government, whether or not the opinions are based on the views of the membership. Which leaders—and which groups—can be regarded as influential? If decision-makers and observers consider a given group as important and if the opinions submitted to government by that group tend to prevail as policy we are entitled to infer that such groups are important in foreign policy-making. We can affirm the existence and prevalence of these processes in American democracy; we cannot assert with precision when and where the influence of any one actor will prevail, though we must review the regularities in public opinion and individual attitudes that do recur.

SOCIETY, ATTITUDES, AND PUBLIC OPINION

Are Americans predisposed toward joining with other nations in common institutions? Studies linking personality with opinion toward isolationism and nonisolationism suggest that Americans are overwhelmingly so disposed and do accept interdependence—at least in the international systems that have prevailed since 1945. Isolationism in modern America is a deviant stance.

The same studies, however, show that "isolationist beliefs are far more common among the general population than they are among the political leaders. Similarly, isolationism is more frequently expressed among the less educated than among the more educated. . . . Isolationism increases as political and social awareness decline: it is more common among the unthinking than among the informed segments of the electorate, stronger among the poor, the culturally deprived, and any other groups who have been cut off from the mainstreams of the articulate culture." [3]

Leaders tend to be less isolationist than the mass of Americans are; Republicans and conservatives are generally more isolationist than are Democrats and liberals. Among political leaders, nonisolationists overwhelmingly favor strengthening the UN, increasing immigration, and relying on military alliances. Isolationist leaders favor decreases in defense spending and foreign aid—an issue on which nonisolationist leaders feel at least ambivalent. Contrast this with opinion at the mass level. Here things cannot be neatly dichotomized; isolationist preferences do not correlate cleanly with unambiguous policy positions, though socioeconomic conservatism on domestic issues does go hand in hand with isolationism.

These findings applied fully to the UN during the 1950's. The educated and higher status groups overwhelmingly supported the UN as a meaningful method of advancing American foreign policy and world peace—though they tended to equate the two. While all strata of the population supported the UN in a general way, only these groups combined knowledge with a deeper commitment and constituted a firm base of supporting opinion.

After 1955 the United States was less and less able to use the UN for the realization of national policy. As the world grew multipolar and as different kinds of power were diffused asymmetrically, the United States had to yield to unfriendly majorities and compromise its preferences on many occasions. Did the legitimacy of the UN in the eyes of the American public suffer as a result? Did the authority of the UN over the will of the informed and concerned American decline, as one might suspect? It did not.

Support for the UN has run far ahead of support for foreign aid, lower tariffs, coexistence with communism, cultural exchange programs! Support for the UN was less and less linked with specific preferences for items in American foreign policy. Since 1960, no less than 92 per cent of the American people have supported the UN, compared to 86 per cent in 1951. Eighty per cent feel the UN is doing a good job and is important to the United States. More than half believe the UN has prevented World War III, and 66 per cent want the UN to have a stronger role in peace-keeping with military forces. In 1966, the 25 per cent who would have admitted Communist China, were an increase from 11 per cent in 1951. Education continued to characterize the most world-minded; but the educated everywhere

[3] Herbert McClosky, "Personality and Attitude Correlates of Foreign Policy Orientation," in J. Rosenau, ed., *Domestic Sources of Foreign Policy* (New York: Free Press, 1967), p. 63.

also manifested a greater readiness to distinguish support for the UN from attitudes on specific international issues, and supporters of the UN were no longer necessarily sanguine that the UN would assure peace and plenty. Further, popular support for the UN was more consistent and stronger than congressional enthusiasm for the world organization. Any significant variation in support for the UN could not, by 1966, be attributed to class, occupation, sex, status, urban or rural residence, or region—with exceptions to be noted.

Although significant regional differences have disappeared, the South continues to be somewhat less reconciled to interdependence than the rest of the country. Moreover, southern opposition to the UN in particular and international cooperation in general has increased in proportion to the intensification of the civil rights struggle. Lower class and lower-middle class people are somewhat more likely to oppose the UN; and among all religions, Jews are most likely to favor it. Negroes, before 1960, tended to be indifferent to UN issues, but since that time have grown to favor the organization.

Since we are concerned with the interplay between the system as seen by the observer and the actor we must be particularly sensitive to shifts in perception and attitude characteristic of different age groups. Do the young see the world and the UN as do the older generations? Are they less or more willing to live in a differently ruled world? As a whole, the young are more willing to give up sovereignty and to make concessions to opinions and demands contrary to American policy. Table 3 recapitulates general shifts in willingness to dismantle the sovereign nation and highlights the views of the young.[4]

Public opinion, then, cannot use specific, consistent terms to tell elites or governments what our foreign policy should be. At best, it forms dikes "which channel public action or which fix a range of discretion within which government may act or within which debate at official levels may proceed."[5] Public opinion defines large substantive areas of consensus that *permit* the government to act and to justify itself after the event. Being permissive, public opinion can be aroused after an action committing the United States has already been taken. Only very rarely—in the field of foreign affairs—does the consensus prohibit the government from taking action.

Gabriel Almond has called the areas of consensus delimited by the dikes of public opinion the "mood" of the American people. That mood is as shallow as the opinions of which it is made up, and as changeable. It fluctuates between the extremes of indifference to foreign affairs and oversimplification of foreign threats, between optimism and pessimism, the desire to withdraw from the web of interdependence and the determination to intervene regularly abroad. The mood wavers between pessimistic and cynical tolerance of other nations and optimistic, idealistic intolerance designed to make the world more American through American aid and sacrifice.

---

[4] Adapted from Hero, "The American Public and the UN, 1954-1966," *op. cit.*
[5] V. O. Key, *Public Opinion and American Democracy* (New York: Knopf, 1961), p. 532.

TABLE 3 · WAYS OF ACHIEVING PEACE

"While everyone seems to agree that peace is an important thing, there are a good many different views as to how to bring it about. Here are some different ideas. . . . Will you . . . tell me which one you come closest to agreeing with?" (From "A Study of Attitudes Concerning Closer Ties Among Democratic Nations." New York: Elmo Roper Assoc., mimeographed, September, 1963, p. vi.)

Selected as best way to bring about peace

	July 1953 (N=3502) Per cent	July 1963 (N=3007) Per cent	July 1963 21-34 yr.-olds Per cent
We shouldn't get tied up in any *more* alliances or joint commitments with other countries, and we should aim at getting out of as many as we can as soon as we can.	9	6	3
We should continue to work along with the United Nations just about as we have been, gradually trying to make it better as time goes on.	21	22	22
We should immediately get behind *strengthening* the United Nations and do everything necessary to give it more power and authority than it has—enough to actually keep even a strong nation from starting a war.	35	39	44
In addition to continuing with the United Nations, we should also unite with the friendly democratic countries into one government in which each member nation would in effect become a state, somewhat like the different states in this country.	6	6	6
We should start now working toward transforming the United Nations into a real world government of *all* nations of the world, in which every nation would in effect become a state, somewhat like the different states in this country.	11	11	13
Some of these ideas are good, but we won't get any of them working in time to prevent war, so we'd better not rely on them.	7	6	6
Don't know or no answer.	11	10	6

Naturally, a sharply experienced crisis can trigger a radical shift i mood. Since many people who support the UN also oppose foreign aid and express a desire to increase domestic welfare without raising taxes, a depression or a war or a housing crisis can possibly trigger an isolationist revival. Intensified racial strife might bring about the same thing. In fact, some contemporary dissenters from the general consensus identify with neither of the two main moods, favoring an active American policy identifying with the revolutionary Third World instead; however, such people are committed to an explicit ideology rather than to a mere mood. A mood, unlike an ideology, hardly provides a firm ground for a consistent policy approved by the public; but it permits leaders great leeway in action and legitimates a broad range of specific steps.

Weak opinions can easily be channeled, if not changed, by strong sources, by persuasive opinion-makers. When President Eisenhower proposed a more active role for the UN, he was heartily applauded by editors, columnists, and TV commentators; but when Nikita Khrushchev proposed the troika formula for the UN, the makers of public comment rallied to the support of the UN as constituted. Leadership and the dissemination of the leader's opinions by the opinion-makers are particularly important in a setting in which shallow and shifting moods account for the bulk of the inattentive public's reaction. Because the moods are shallow they respond to manipulation by respected authorities. Hence we turn to a discussion of elites, interest groups, and foreign policy.

INTEREST GROUPS, ELITES, AND POLITICS

That America is a nation of joiners has been known for some time. Those who join together for organized political action belong to the genus "interest group"; but the *scope, intensity* and *duration* of their effective interests vary. We know little that is systematic and beyond question about interest group influence on foreign policy, but let us list what we do know.

Most familiar are the large civic, fraternal, and educational groups intended to be permanent and to devote their attention to a very wide spectrum of issues, ranging from local charity and improvement to the UN and world peace. The wider the spectrum of their concern, the lower is the intensity of their attention for any one issue. The League of Women Voters is rarely successful in organizing a local community on single foreign policy issues, such as the 1962 Trade Expansion Act. The American Association of University Women maintains national and local committees on legislation; but they are rarely heard, even though they stand for a clear policy in favor of a strong UN. The American Legion has failed for decades in trying to make the government downgrade the UN. Masons, Elks, Rotarians number many millions of Americans among their members, but their size and diversity of interests condemn these organizations to a passive role in foreign policy-making.

These are the groups that contain the local "notables" of American politics. People with status, education, and concern—the attention public—

ᴎerally belong to such groups. They respond first to appeals coming from ᴖe government; they join the special committees and commissions designed ᴑ arouse public concern when Washington considers a major shift in foreign policy; they are the prime recipients and participants in a *downward* flow of influence. On the other hand, they may also influence that policy by virtue of their membership on the major citizens advisory bodies associated with government programs, such as the Freedom from Hunger Foundation or the General Advisory Committee of the U.S. Arms Control and Disarmament Agency. Their beliefs cluster at the internationalist end of the attitude spectrum.

Groups of notables tend to facilitate government initiatives rather than launch innovations of their own. A second type of group, however, does take the initiative. Here we think of multipurpose organizations of a permanent nature or "attention groups" that experience an intense commitment to certain single issues. Predominantly, this includes American religious bodies and ethnic groups. The Ancient Order of Hibernians is not greatly interested in foreign policy unless the issue of Ulster is raised. American Jews focus on the UN only when Israel and the fate of Jews abroad seem to matter. The Catholic Church is active in foreign affairs—as an organized group—only when the issue seems to be atheistic communism. The American Friends Service Committee is particularly active when the issue is one of international understanding and conciliation. Groups of this character include notables and local elites. They are sometimes of crucial importance in initiating and demanding specific *single* actions or bills in Washington, but not in consistent and long-range foreign affairs activity.

Thirdly, we have the major economic and occupational interest groups. They are permanent organizations, with the single major purpose of advancing the economic well-being of workers, farmers, businessmen or professional people, and an intense commitment to those aspects of foreign policy that are related to the main organizational purpose. Like the civic and fraternal groups, their leaders are part of the elite that has access to government and communicates between the mass membership and the inattentive public, on the one hand, and the makers of policy, on the other. Like the notables, leaders of these interest groups are the nongovernmental elites of American society who participate in fashioning the public consensus in support of policy; unlike those leaders, they take a continuous and active part in initiating suggestions and demands for policy.

These groups display more of an ideological structure in their approach than do unorganized individuals or multipurpose organizations, though they are not typically rigid. The American Federation of Labor–Congress of Industrial Organizations has supported a militant anticommunist policy but is also committed to the stimulation of free trade unions abroad, cast in the pluralist mold. The National Students Association has generally supported government policy, though it has demanded stronger and more radical steps in favor of decolonization and human rights in Africa and Latin America—blaming the United States for faltering in this area. The major business groups—U.S. National Chamber of Commerce, National Association of Manufacturers, Committee for Economic Development—have

all supported the general line of policy since 1945, including increas
participation in the UN and other international organizations. Regardr
general policy these groups are not necessarily significant or powerful.

Their influence is much stronger on specific issues, such as a fisherie
agreement, tariff negotiations, immigration of farm labor, and certain aspects
of foreign aid (e.g., the rule that half of American aid must be shipped on
American vessels). Here, influence can be attributed to the fact that congressmen and administrative officials close to the group's concerns are
accessible to lobbying and that these policy-makers sometimes depend on
information and arguments from the lobbyists for their ammunition. Further,
the demands are often precise, clearly linked to the welfare of an identifiable
group or voting bloc, and not really contested by any other group. Under
those circumstances specific economic group demands can often see enactment. Yet on other, or more general, issues the same groups are powerless
because neither ,congressmen nor administrators need pay any attention to
them.

Businessmen tend to be more and more committed to freer trade and
to international competition, an attitude that is correlated with a belief that
an open world and an open United States contribute to strengthening
democracy at the expense of communism. The larger and better-informed
business groups and firms display these commitments to a greater extent
than the smaller ones. Yet even these "people fail to see where their self-
interest lies." [6]

The assessments and calculations of single-purpose interest groups are
couched in immediate short-run terms; they are seldom based on careful
analysis, even when they are made by groups with intense, focused commitments. American interest groups—whether business or labor—are far from
constituting a single-minded, powerful, and consistent bloc in favor of free
enterprise and anticommunism.

Our final type of interest group differs from the three we have an-
alyzed, in that its members usually are part of the opposition to government policy and that its leaders are not typically part of the opinion-
making elites who occupy powerful positions in American life. We here
deal with single-purpose groups of intense commitment, usually temporary
in nature and organized around a single, burning issue. United World
Federalists (membership: 20,000) is such a group. The China Lobby of the
1940's was another one. At the end of the 1930's two *ad hoc* groupings
opposed each other actively: one determined to keep the United States out
of World War II, the other determined to intervene on the side of Britain
and France. The isolationist grouping tended to be the political "outs." The
interventionists—in this instance—were broadly representative of the urban
notables and important economic interest groups. They sought to influence
Washington in favor of intervention and the government gladly availed
itself of the group's resources and prestige, to steer the country toward
involvement, to exploit the shallow and diffuse mood prevailing at that
time. In the late 1960's, the Peace Movement is the most significant grouping
of this type.

[6] Raymond A. Bauer, Ithiel de S. Pool, and Lewis A. Dexter, *American Business
and Public Policy* (New York: Atherton, 1963), p. 128.

As long as the movement simply sought to prepare antigovernment statements and projects and present these directly to policy-makers, very little attention was paid to its efforts. These demands hinged mostly around disarmament, opposition to racial discrimination abroad, and the encouragement of "popular" regimes in Africa and Latin America. Much of the effort became irrelevant with the arms control agreements accepted by the super-powers and the end of colonialism (except in southern Africa). Even the World Federalists merely advocated piecemeal reform—the establishment of the Arms Control Agency, repeal of the Connally reservation, more financial support for the UN—and ran out of steam when many of them were enacted. The Peace Movement, however, regained relevance to foreign policy-making when the Vietnam war became the central issue and tactics changed to mass action at the local level, including civil disobedience and violence. The effort was designed to fuse commitment to civil rights, pacifism, "people's liberation from imperialism," Negro nationalism, and general left-wing opposition to the style of American politics—and to fuse them at the mass level. Foreign policy became *the* issue on which disaffected groups sought to build a coalition of opposition forces, thus running counter to the pluralist-elitist flavor of public opinion and interest group action in the foreign-policy field. If the Peace Movement were to succeed, it would be the first time in American history that an *ad hoc* group of intense commitment—not part of the circle of regularly participating elites—signally affected the course of policy.

What about the military in this array of publics and groups? It is sometimes argued that the military constitutes an interest group of its own, advocating and implementing policy to protect its investment in weapons systems, strategic ideas, and foreign enemies—thus protecting its status and prestige in American life. It is undeniable that military experts do suggest strategies and influence decisions opting for this weapons system or that, thus committing the country to new strategies. Further, the identity of present and future enemies may be left to the judgment of the military professionals. The facts that we possess, however, suggest that the military is divided internally, that services squabble over strategies, missions, and weapons and that they do not necessarily see eye to eye on the character of the enemy. Even though the public is certainly excluded from military-political decisions, there is a great measure of internal pluralism among military organizations and among their civilian superiors, thus arguing against the unambiguous dominance of an "industrial-military complex."

Do businessmen or Protestants or Irishmen run American foreign policy? No single group—and no coalition—seems to be predictably influential on more than a single issue. All groups are more or less ineffective, unless welded into a special coalition for a great purpose consistent with the ideological commitments of the major elites and the government. Even business groups, which are the most effective of all the organizations we have surveyed, "are nevertheless only mildly influential and then only with respect to a rather narrow range of economic issues which comprise only a small proportion of the fundamental issues of American foreign policy." We see little hint of domination when we observe the successful efforts of a single-purpose, small and focused interest group, such as the Pacific Coast fisheries industry, to insert clauses favorable to it in a peace treaty. Indeed, the very flow of communications and messages is so complex and runs in so many diverse directions that the policy-maker is bombarded with not one set of demands or ideas, but with a plurality of clashing ones. The access of interest groups, in turn, is a competitive phenomenon. One group must fight with others for time; indeed, some studies suggest that interest groups spend a great deal of time seeking merely to arouse their own members to put pressure on the policy-maker. Many congressmen deliberately expose themselves to a cacophony of ideas through questionnaires addressed to their constituents or through community conferences held for them.

As for interest groups and the UN, the record shows the institutional logic of imperfect pluralism at work. For some years a Conference Group of national organizations attempted to speak for all major interests on matters relating to the UN. The Conference Group spoke for large, permanent, single-interest groups as well as for the larger multipurpose groupings, in addition to some *ad hoc* organizations. Since the UN was the only common denominator among the interests represented, the denominator was so low that it precluded effective action—and the Conference Group languished. Diverse membership implies diffuseness and lack of power. No single interest is triumphant; indeed, it would be more accurate to say that neither individual attitudes nor organized groups shape foreign policy in any regularly discernible fashion. Is there, then, a power elite that links the government to key persons in society and in the economy and is it this elite that runs things?

GOVERNMENT, BUREAUCRACY, AND THE PRESIDENT

"In the realm of foreign policy there has not been a single major issue on which Presidents, when they were serious and determined, have failed." [7] An examination of how foreign policy decisions have been made over the last quarter of a century will permit no other conclusion. But how can that be, when Congress has the power to vote or withhold appropriations for all foreign and defense programs, when the Senate must approve treaties by a two-thirds majority, and when the committees of both Houses can, and do, investigate the operations of the Executive in foreign affairs? How can the President—as a person—dominate so completely when he has the State and Defense departments as expert assistants, the National Security Council, the Joint Chiefs of Staff, and the foreign policy demands of less involved agencies such as the Atomic Energy Commission and the Departments of Labor and Agriculture? How can one man prevail over several armies of specialists and professionals in foreign and defense questions?

Let us examine the presidential dominance thesis first with respect to Congress. Table 4 shows the degree of presidential success in dealing with Congress. But we cannot assume that Congress *wishes* to oppose the Presi-

[7] Aaron Wildavsky, "The Two Presidencies." Copyright © 1966 by Washington University, St. Louis, Mo. Reprinted from *Trans-action* magazine (December, 1966), p. 7.

TABLE 4 · CONGRESSIONAL ACTION ON PRESIDENTIAL PROPOSALS
FROM 1948 to 1964

Policy area	Congressional action		Number of proposals
	% Passed	% Failed	
Domestic policy (natural resources, labor, agriculture, taxes, etc.)	40.2	59.8	2499
Defense policy (defense, disarmament, manpower, misc.)	73.3	26.7	90
Foreign policy	58.5	41.5	655
Immigration, refugees	13.2	86.0	129
Treaties, general foreign relations, State Department, foreign aid	70.8	29.2	445

Source: Aaron Wildavsky, "The Two Presidencies." Copyright © 1966 by Washington University, St. Louis, Mo. Reprinted from *Trans-action* magazine (December, 1966).

dent. Though the President must evaluate the likelihood of congressional opposition to his plans—and in this sense Congress has a deterrent effect—the legislators on the *whole* and as a *bloc* do not wish to oppose him or detract from his leadership. Still, individual senators commonly oppose him; occasionally a congressional committee or a strong minority on it takes the initiative in blocking or criticizing an aspect of foreign policy. But as long as the President vigorously fights for his preferences, these challenges rarely succeed.

The normal play of party politics, in short, does not operate clearly and consistently in foreign policy-making. The two major parties do not frontally and consistently disagree on foreign and defense policy questions. There is, at the center of the political spectrum in Congress, a considerable overlap among liberal Republicans and the bulk of northeastern moderate Democrats, and this coalition has provided the "foreign policy consensus" in the last twenty years. Neither party is a disciplined entity and prolonged negotiations within each party are necessary before the party caucus takes a firm position. Thus a skillful President can rule with the help of shifting coalitions of party factions; his manipulative talents can exploit congressional incoherence, division, and desire to defer to a more knowing source of information. This means that conservative Republicans and southern Democrats who advocate some version of withdrawal from, or all-out offensive in, world affairs have been more or less consistently deprived of influence. It also means that radical Democrats who favor retrenchment in military affairs and a foreign policy exclusively dedicated to "peace" have suffered the same fate.

There are several reasons for this nonpartisanship. Congressmen, as a rule, are under minimal pressure from their constituents on questions of foreign policy, thus permitting each legislator to vote as he pleases or respond to presidential initiatives. This naturally gives respected experts or persuasive advocates greater influence than they have on many domestic issues. It is true, as former Secretary of State Dean Acheson said, that administration officials spend as much as one-sixth of their time appearing before congressional committees to explain and advocate foreign policy measures. While the President's men must justify themselves continuously, they almost always have their way.

Although congressional committees have been accommodating in accepting administration requests for regional and collective security measures, there are nevertheless some sharp limits to congressional compliance. The formidable Joint Committee on Atomic Energy has gone its own way, and the administration has respected its autonomy by seeking to avoid international nuclear steps that would require the committee's approval. Congress has rarely disputed the creation of new international organizations or America's membership in them. Nor have the legislators as a group quarreled with the principle of foreign aid, bilateral or multilateral. They have, however, balked sharply at the amounts of aid, the sums contributed by the United States to international organizations, and the creation of world trade rules considered to impinge on congressional prerogatives with respect to tariff policy. We will note these limits on American learning and participation later. Congressional insistence on financial caution in supporting international commitments is clearly apparent in the oft-asserted rule that the United States provide no more than a fixed share of the budgets of the United Nations system—ranging between 32 and 50 per cent—and in the sharp cuts in foreign aid appropriations imposed by Congress on the President in recent years. But this limit on presidential leadership tends to operate without party influence.

The State and Defense departments have more than one million civilian officials. Do these men, then, make the policies that re-enforce, confirm, or destroy the web of interdependence? In a general way, the answer is "yes." Initial thought about what future policy should be and what immediate measures should be taken to implement existing policy does come from these departments in the Executive Branch. But they have their way only if the President and his personal staff do *not* have ideas and wishes of their own. Presidents can, and do, override, outflank, and ignore their Secretaries of State; they direct and prod the Foreign Service and the military services —and they play them off against each other on occasion. Since 1952, at any rate, the persons who have held the offices of President, Secretary of State, and Secretary of Defense at any one time have been so close to each other in values and judgment that little occasion for conflict arose.

Are the two giant departments monoliths of bureaucrats who go their own professionally-sanctioned ways when permitted to do so by the President? Public *control* over either is absent; but *consultations* with the public are routine. Thus the State Department carefully follows press and public opinion on foreign affairs questions. Its officials routinely talk to representatives of interest groups. In addition, panels of distinguished private experts are consulted by the professionals in government. None of this is true in the same way of the Department of Defense or the Central Intelligence Agency. Occasionally, conflict among officials is "resolved" by referring a question of high strategy to a panel of distinguished private citizens. Technical studies of alternative strategies are undertaken by civilian research institutes related to the department. And representatives of armaments firms of course regularly seek to influence the department in favor of this or that weapons system. By and large Defense goes its own professionally-sanctioned way, subject only to the will of the President. As for the CIA, only major failures in operations exposed fully its freedom from control.

We must add, finally, that certain private interests exercise an inordinate amount of influence on certain other departments of government marginally related to foreign affairs. Thus organized labor is most important in shaping the position of the Department of Labor with respect to international issues; farmers' organizations are equally powerful in using the Department of Agriculture in this way.

What about the Joint Chiefs of Staff and the National Security Council? Doesn't the prestige of these organs predetermine the President's choices? The Joint Chiefs scrupulously avoid making firm recommendations; instead, they tend to adopt resolutions with generalities that simply plaster over interservice disagreements. Even when they do make firm recommendations, the President does not necessarily accept them; Eisenhower, for example, ignored the Joint Chiefs' recommendation to intervene in the 1954 Indochina war. The National Security Council, the President's chief advisory body on foreign and defense matters, groups all the cabinet officials concerned, as well as the Central Intelligence Agency. The consensus of observers is that the council is little more than a forum for negotiating interagency differences; furthermore, Presidents vary in the extent to which they use the council. The President makes policy, essentially, on the basis of direct access to him, open to crucial officials in the two main departments. There is no firm military policy determined by professionals on "rational" or technical grounds; there is only interservice and interagency bargaining using all the normal political techniques for attracting allies and building coalitions—so long as the President has not made up his own mind on what course to follow.

All roads of inquiry, then, lead to the President as the fountainhead of foreign-policy-making power. This power, first of all, does have the sanction of the Constitution. In addition, the diffuse state of public opinion and the incoherence of interest group activity, coupled with the willingness of Congress to be led on foreign-policy questions, provide the President with the political setting in which to exercise his constitutional powers. The fact of the matter, of course, is that some Presidents seize the opportunity consistently and others do not. Strong leadership appeals to the public; the skillful use of the press and television, energetic nonpartisan persuasion of Congress usually bring acquiescence to the policy desired by a President; the failure to exercise leadership results in widespread attack and opposition. The election in which a foreign-policy issue defeated the governing party —the contest of 1952 and the Korean war—illustrates this rule: a confused and divided electorate mirrors an equally confused and irresolute Administration's policy. An active President remains abreast of public moods by means of polls and surveys; he seeks to shape the moods through press conferences and television appearances. A passive President neglects these channels and pays the price in opposition. Both kinds suffer from public ill will if they are unable to shape a coherent and understandable policy, to be clearly communicated to the people. And such is the mood of the American public that neither an active nor a passive President can long have his way unless the policy he follows appears to be successful. Prolonged sacrifices will not be tolerated by the American public unless visible success attends them.

This discussion suggests that presidential leadership is restrained only by the natural limits of the chief executive's energy and motivation. Additionally, perhaps, the entrenched bureaucratic power and *expertise* of federal agencies act as a brake on presidential initiatives. Each agency, being a complex organization in its own right, tends to act as a self-sufficient, goal-seeking, goal-attaining unit with needs and demands of its own, not subject to simple control by way of presidential wish or formal interagency coordinating machinery. How then can we conceptualize more formal limits on presidential power? A survey of the *types of decisions* Presidents must make will help matters, as will a look at the *kind of consensus* required to make such decisions effective. We distinguish between emergency decisions, the initiation of major new programs, and the evaluation of ongoing policy.

Emergency decisions are made in secret by the President's closest collaborators: the White House staff, the Secretaries of State and Defense, the Director of CIA. Such decisions may, and do, involve war and peace, the use of nuclear weapons, escalation and de-escalation, appeals to the UN or to NATO, interpreting ambiguous radar blips, extending emergency aid to an attacked nation, recognizing or not recognizing a regime resulting from a coup or a revolution abroad. They must be made rapidly, and they require immediate and coordinated implementation. No consensus outside the inner circle can be built. If the decisions made require money and lives and if success is not rapidly achieved, this very lack of consensus may spell the failure of the decision, particularly when it runs counter to the prevalent public mood.

Major new policies are discussed in the public arena, which includes Congress, the press, interest groups, and the whole attentive public. Major new policies usually demand additional resources, financial and human. Money must be appropriated, new missions abroad constituted, thinking patterns changed. Consensual bridges among all parties affected become essential. A President eager to launch such a program must build coalitions of supporters in the interest group and congressional world if he wishes to succeed. Major new programs, then, are in effect negotiated among all parties concerned before being formally voted on by Congress. The terms of major departures such as the Marshall Plan, the Alliance for Progress, and NATO are defined through the process of bargaining, because they trigger group, class, and regional interests that demand a hearing and that command votes. Experts make recommendations and studies, but these are filtered through the prism of intergroup and interparty bargains; they do not stand on their professional merits alone. Congress therefore often ignores and counters the President's suggestions in the politics of approving foreign

d and defense production—*unless* the President has taken care to build
ie proper supporting coalitions with appropriate package deals. Opposition
.o foreign aid has grown quite consistently since 1961, a trend matched by
increasing lack of cohesion and agreement among executive departments
dealing with foreign aid. The larger the programs have grown, the more
opposition and greater lack of administrative focus have developed, as
segments of the public and of government have been pitted against each
other to see who gets what and how much.

But the President's own executive agencies can give him plenty of
trouble on the way. "Officialdom, whether civil or military, is hardly ever
neutral. It speaks, and inevitably, it speaks as an advocate. The Army battles
for ground forces, the Air Force for bombers, the 'Europe faction' in the
State Department for policy benefiting NATO, and the 'Africa faction' for
anti-colonial policies unsettling to our relations with Europe." [8] The result
is "policy" only in the sense that continuing bargaining and negotiation
among executive agencies eventually result in a compromise among them.
Not even the best-informed and strongest-willed President can impose his
own preferences unless he can be sure that his decision will be faithfully
and rapidly carried out. There is very little planning of policy in Washington. Policy emerges incrementally, step-by-step, from crisis to crisis, as a
result of interagency confrontation and compromise mediated by the President. Hence it is of the greatest importance to the representative principle
in American government that the leaders of executive agencies, the major
"front men" of Washington, be people who command confidence and fol-
lowers among important interest groups, whether they be "liberals" like
Adlai Stevenson and Arthur Goldberg or "conservatives" with ties in law,
business, and industry like John McCone, John J. McCloy, or Dean Acheson.
A President legitimates his leadership over his own agencies by staffing them
with such front men. He limits the interagency conflict and bargaining by
this technique.

Decisions involving evaluation are semipublic. Typically, they involve
high-level presidential commissions or panels charged with evaluating the
success of past policies and making suggestions for the future. Initially,
these steps are secret. But as the results come to affect competing federal
agencies, leaks to the public occur and the President's final choice is influenced by the expectations and fears aroused by these unauthorized dis-
closures.

If funds and much new thought are involved in implementing a new
policy, the President is constrained to build supporting coalitions in Congress and in the interest-group world. Moreover, he must still persuade his
federal agencies to do his bidding, though he usually attempts to do this in
the first place by including their representatives on the commission. Organizational structures brought into being by earlier, important departures
from policy—like the various foreign aid agencies and various divisions of
departments dealing with specific international organizations—now become
defenders of the *status quo* and must be negotiated with before another
new departure in policy can be undertaken. This process is illustrated by

[8] Roger Hilsman, *To Move a Nation* (Garden City, N.Y.: Doubleday, 1967), p. 8.

studies and negotiations in Washington leading to the creation of foreig
aid programs, civilian defense outlays, strategic missile planning, and th
use of subversion abroad.

DEMOCRACY AND FOREIGN-POLICY MAKING

Policy, then, is incremental. It "is made" by moving from package deal
to package deal without much thought for an over-all scheme, a total design
that takes in immediate crises, intermediate trends, and long-range probable
developments in the broad field of human ecology. And thus policy is
always an approximation of rational and comprehensive thought, just as it
is merely an approximation of a pure pluralistic democratic pattern.

In fact, it has been argued that the process is not democratic at all,
because it does not provide for consistent mass or elite participation. To
argue thus is to insist on procedures that presume equal commitment, intelligence, and knowledge on the part of all the people. Alternatively, it
would give disproportionate powers to the minority that actually has these
attributes, rather than to the people's elected representatives and to the
professional specialists chosen on the basis of their competence. Pluralism,
though imperfect, remains democratic as long as the leaders must bargain
for support among the elites and the public, and as long as segments of
the public have the ability to influence policy by means of access to the
bureaucracy. Shallow as the public mood may be the fact that it does act
as a constraint on leadership confirms the persistence of popular force. But
as long as the mood remains shallow, arguments in favor of better and more
profound modes of public participation in policy-making are more likely to
result in more effective downward manipulation than in genuine and informed democratic control from below. If the power elite model gives a
grotesquely inaccurate picture of American policy-making, the pure democratic model yields a house built on sand.

When America learns to adapt to new complications abroad and
fashions new strands in the web of interdependence, the learning most
often originates in the bureaucracy and among those elites who experience
the international system most profoundly, such as industrialists, bankers,
lawyers, and cultural leaders. Overwhelmingly, foreign events, not domestic
trends and crises, have caused an American adaptation. It was not the Depression that turned America toward intervention in the late 1930's.

But the late 1960's taught us the limits of this rule: when painful
failure abroad combines with massive domestic crises such as racial in-
surrection, the decay of cities, and large-scale unemployment, a change in
foreign policy *can* be attributed to essentially domestic events. Dissenters
from the ongoing foreign policy use these events to impress upon policy-
makers the connections between failures at home and abroad. The government's response in terms of new policy then constitutes adaptive learning,
forced by a new coalition of domestic political forces. Congress may come
into its own again. So may leaders who were not previously part of the
inner policy-making circle.

Yet, while such learning does occur, it is just as piecemeal and incremental as the previous round of learning. The dissenters will succeed in teaching the government that it is impossible to have both guns and butter, to fight costly wars abroad and improve the fundamental conditions of twenty million people at home. But they will fail in having butter take the place of guns. They will make us question the rules of the international system and challenge us to fit together many new pieces in the jigsaw puzzle of policy. But will the search for a more tolerable international system result in a dramatic breakthrough? Even if incrementalism makes possible such drastic changes, should we look for them and welcome them indiscriminately?

3

National Security,
World Peace, and Disarmament

Webs are made up of single strands. In world politics, the strands include the search for military and political security through the United Nations and through regional alliances and treaty organizations—though it is not always clear whether we are talking of the world's security or America's. Another and closely related strand is the attempt to abolish, limit, or control armaments. Efforts to spur and support the economic development of the impoverished two-thirds of the world spin a constantly thickening strand: Some of these efforts are made by the UN and its specialized agencies; others are the preserve of the Organization for Economic Cooperation and Development (OECD) and the Organization of American States (OAS). Further, the rules governing world trade, competition, access to foreign markets, lending, borrowing, and monetary policy constitute an area of obvious interdependence in which UN agencies are important actors. The international protection of human rights and the abolition of the colonial system are twin objectives and activities that have generated strands of interdependence in recent years. The United Nations is the chief actor here, too. Finally, the scientific and technological breakthroughs are becoming increasingly important in international life because they suggest perhaps new, improved ways of doing things while also propelling us toward new and more frightening challenges to an orderly and humane world. We must inquire whether the possible consequences of such breakthroughs, unintended by governments and elites, may not lead to a species of worldwide planning that might fundamentally transform the character of the web.

These are the strands of the web in which the United States and all other countries, in varying degrees, are enmeshed if not entrapped. Clearly, when the outlines of the contemporary system took shape in the minds of Western policy-makers in 1945 these issues and concerns were not all intended or foreseen. The unity of the big powers after 1945 was soon replaced by the bipolar confrontation we know as the Cold War. Bipolarity, after 1955, gave way to multipolarity with the advent of new nations and their demands for economic betterment, decolonization, and military nonalignment. The period since 1955 is our major concern in this book. We wish to know *how* the United States adjusted to the multipolar world and its multiplying issue areas and concerns. We want to know *what* the United States learned that kept it from leaving the system that had failed fully to contain communism and preserve the *status quo* of 1945.

WORLD PEACE AND AMERICAN SECURITY IN THE BIPOLAR SYSTEM

In the wake of World War II, the victor powers set up the UN to prevent a repetition of the violent tragedies that had engulfed the world since the middle of the 1930's. There cannot be the slightest doubt that the American people, in the mass and in opinion-making groups, gave overwhelming support to the idea of a world organization with peacekeeping power. Majorities in excess of 70 per cent in 1944 and 1945 favored an organization with power to stop all wars, to fix the military power of individual nations, earmark national forces for global peacekeeping, decide on the merits of disputes between nations, make binding laws, and even examine schoolbooks to eliminate nationalist biases.

These opinions—subject to all the strictures set forth in Chapter 2 about the role of public opinion—were expressed while the the war was still in progress. A few years later, the internationalist ardor of the American public had cooled a bit. The change is reported in the most comprehensive study of this period:

> When support for the United Nations is presented without reference to other means of maintaining peace and security, a large majority [of the people interviewed] is in favor of it. When presented as an alternative to other policies, sizable proportions of people continue to advocate support for the United Nations, but the alternatives of strengthening US defenses and developing separate alliances with friendly nations attract about as many advocates.[1]

The decline of enthusiasm for UN peacekeeping efforts coincides with the intensification of the Cold War after 1948. But in the immediate aftermath of World War II even the American Legion, always concerned with stressing the unique role of American armed forces in maintaining peace, strongly favored the UN and saw in it the forum for the deployment of American troops. In 1947, when President Truman bypassed the UN in

[1] William A. Scott and Stephen B. Withey, *The United States and the United Nations* (New York: Manhattan Publishing Co., 1958), p. 23.

TABLE 5 · *CHOICE OF ALTERNATIVE*
U.S. FOREIGN POLICIES (NORC) IN PER CENTS

	1949 Nov.	1950 June	1950 July	1951 Mar.
United States should rely mainly on:				
The United Nations Organization and do what it can to make it more effective	28	27	40	32
Alliances with other democratic countries, and work toward closer unity with them	27	35	30	31
Its own armed forces, and stay out of world affairs as much as possible	38	32	26	30
No opinion	7	6	4	7

Source: National Opinion Research Center. Quoted in Scott and Withey, *The United States and the United Nations*, p. 24.

coming to the aid of Greece and Turkey, 66 per cent of the public disapproved and 51 per cent thought the UN was able to cope with the situation. Why, then, did not the government, fully and without reservation, combine the American desire for peace with the work of the UN?

Obviously, the government did not think that the UN could handle the situation. That, however, is another way of saying that measures undertaken by the UN would not have been in the national interest. Policy in international organizations is still part of national policy, usually only a subordinate part at that. United States foreign policy uses purely national initiatives—military, economic, cultural, and diplomatic—alongside multilateral steps through regional organizations as well as the UN. The calculation of whether to use the UN as the mainstay of policy involves (1) the types of action the UN can take, (2) the type of military confrontation which the action is to meet and control and (3) the price of a UN operation in terms of international consensus. We know that such calculations conform to the type of international system in which the country finds itself, whether bipolar, multipolar or multibloc. The United States never deliberately defined her interests as being identical with the success of the UN, but the process of learning taught Washington how to mix UN objectives with America's in everchanging proportions as the bipolar system gave way to the multibloc world. In fact, the learning changed the system.

The Charter to which the world agreed in 1945 banned the use of force and the threat of it in international relations and guaranteed each member nation its territorial integrity and security. How? Two types of action were enumerated in the Charter; a third developed immediately in practice. Elaborate procedures for peacefully settling disputes among nations are prescribed, using the Security Council as well as the General

Assembly. These procedures involve the collective mediation and conciliation of the UN between antagonists, but they are not binding on them. In the event of a breach of the peace or act of aggression in defiance of "peaceful settlement" procedures, the UN is able to order binding "enforcement" measures, military as well as nonmilitary, against the guilty state. But as the Kashmir (1947), Palestine (1948), and Indonesian (1949) cases soon demonstrated, a third way of keeping the peace was the establishment of a truce by order of the Security Council and the creation of neutral forces for "truce supervision," a step short of enforcement. Enforcement was ordered by the Security Council only once, ineffectively against Rhodesia in 1966. "Peacekeeping" by means of forces temporarily contributed by small countries and placed under UN command seeks to separate the combatants physically and contain them without forcing the peacekeepers to fight. This is a development not foreseen in the Charter and improvised by the Secretary-General under the very different conditions of the multipolar system that made its advent after 1955.

When do the members reach agreement on which kind of action to take? Before we reply, the various types of possible military confrontations should be set forth. The most general type of confrontation conceivable is a general thermonuclear war between the Western and Communist blocs; this type is by definition beyond the scope of UN action since the countries designed to guarantee peace under the Charter would then become the antagonists that call peace into question. A limited war between the two camps, on the other hand, might be amenable to UN intercession, and a limited war among other countries certainly should be amenable to intercession. The same is true of small and carefully controlled probing attacks designed to test the enemy's strength and will to resist. Local wars fought by nations outside the major ideological camps contribute heavily to the number of actual military conflicts; when these are in danger of escalating into larger conflicts they become natural targets of UN action and concern. Some local wars, however, are so far removed from becoming sources of escalation or general concern that neither the great powers nor the UN is likely to be able to intercede successfully, because nobody is sufficiently concerned to make the necessary effort. Finally, there is the type of conflict we call "internal war," or civil strife tied to international ideological conflict and indirectly supported from the outside. This type of conflict is not "aggression" in the sense of the UN Charter, and it presents some of the chief difficulties in the decision of whether to use the UN or sidestep it in the attainment of a national objective.

But who would provide the counterforce needed for UN action? In 1945 the maintenance of peace and security was lodged in the Security Council in which each of the major nations—United States, Soviet Union, France, Britain and China—has the power to veto a resolution: the major powers have to be unanimously in favor of a given course of action before anything can be done to stop aggression. Since nobody expected the great powers themselves to submit voluntarily to being policed by their peers, this meant that the machinery could work only if war was threatened by a smaller nation. In short, the security of mankind depended on the maintenance of a concert of confidence and power among the large nations. The institutional and symbolic proof of this understanding lay in the fact that the military enforcement machinery of the UN—the stillborn Military Staff Committee and national forces earmarked for its use—was to be made up entirely of personnel furnished by the major powers. By 1948 the basic assumptions underlying a successful functioning of the UN were no longer met, the Cold War was under way, and the implication was that a "concert" of the major powers could be effectively mobilized only in conflicts of a local nature. If the conflicts did not involve the interests or direct commitments of Washington, Moscow, London, or Paris, the UN Security Council could continue to work. There were as many such conflicts then as there are now, and the cease-fires and truce supervision procedures adopted in the Middle East, South and Southeast Asia illustrate the continued importance of a big power consensus that could prevail despite, or because of, the Cold War.

In crises involving a direct confrontation with communism, however, the Security Council was deadlocked, and UN action became impossible. The United States, disappointed with the built-in limits of the UN machinery, looked for ways to use its majority in the world body to subject the Soviet Union itself—though one of the original guarantors of world peace —to the enforcement procedure. It did so by bypassing the Security Council and relying on a two-thirds majority in the vetoless General Assembly instead. Such a majority could *recommend,* not order, enforcement and other security measures, and the recommendation would then lend the UN's mantle of legitimacy to the military operations undertaken by the member nations. The United States government, encouraged by the undifferentiated and shallowly held public view supporting the UN, thus "learned" to adapt the rules of the world organization to suit the anti-Soviet purposes of American foreign policy. The Greek and Korean interventions authorized by the United Nations followed. By 1950 the UN seemed to have become an instrument of United States policy in the pursuit of the Cold War. But instead of the Charter-sanctioned consensual principle for enforcement action, the new principle involved simply the delegation of enforcement power by the UN majority to the United States and its allies. Enforcement, instead of being collective and binding, became permissive and selective.

But only so long as the UN forces in Korea were winning. As soon as China entered that conflict and threatened to trigger American escalation, the bulk of the UN membership sought to limit the anti-Communist mandate earlier given the United States. The bipolar confrontation that had prevailed between 1948 and 1951 altered as an Arab-Asian grouping of states mediated between the two poles, using the UN as a balancer between hostile blocs rather than as an enforcement agency. And thus a new consensual principle evolved *ad hoc:* the negotiation through parliamentary diplomacy in the General Assembly of a compromise agreement between the antagonists, even though one fought under the UN flag, a process we label "balancing." The principle could be successfully used to end the fighting of localized and probing wars among the major powers and their allies. It could not be used, any more than any other consensual principle, to end direct and major military confrontations among the large powers.

NATIONAL SECURITY, WORLD PEACE,
AND THE MULTIPOLAR SYSTEM

In 1955, Washington and Moscow negotiated a "package deal" by virtue of which sixteen additional nations were admitted to UN membership, seven of them not allied to either East or West. By 1958, six more nonaligned nations had been admitted. By 1966, forty more new nations were members, all but four or five nonaligned. The United States, because of the procedures on enforcement of security used in the Greek and Korean cases, had committed itself to upgrade sharply the peace maintenance powers of the General Assembly. More nonaligned members meant more restraints on America's ability to manipulate the UN procedures. The original lesson learned—upgrading the General Assembly at the expense of the veto-bound Security Council—produced unintended results in that the American freedom of maneuver was once more circumscribed by an unreliable majority. How, if at all, would the United States adapt to this new environment in its pursuit of the containment policy through the UN?

It bears stressing that the UN by no means always facilitated the attainment of American foreign policy objectives in the years since the bipolar world broke up. In 1956 the UN failed in stopping Soviet intervention in Hungary; nor did it resolve the Suez Canal crisis fully in line with American preferences. In 1958 the UN operated at cross purposes with American objectives in Lebanon. In 1960 operations in the Congo did not always correspond to United States policy, though they did in 1962. The Cuban missile crisis of 1962 was resolved without UN help, even though mediatory services were proffered. Opponents of American policies in the Western Hemisphere sought to use the UN to counter American measures in Panama (1964) and the Dominican Republic (1965). Communist and nonaligned states attempted to oppose American policy in Vietnam on several occasions, and Secretary-General U Thant, in 1965 and 1966, sought to mediate that war without American encouragement. In short, the UN increasingly appeared as an opponent rather than as an instrument of the national interest as defined by the government.

Did the public perceive, approve or condemn this changed role? The American public, by almost uniform two-thirds majorities, recorded its approval of UN peacekeeping operations since 1956, even advocating the creation of strong, standing, peacekeeping contingents not under American control. Approval was expressed even at times of setbacks suffered by UN forces and by American policy. Furthermore, general expressions of opinion more and more saw the UN as the proper agency for dealing with "brush fire wars," local conflicts not related to the Cold War or other big power confrontations. The reduced military participation of the large powers in UN peacekeeping operations was apparently welcomed by the public. Again, therefore, the mood and elite perceptions of the national interest proved permissive, allowing the government to take new initiatives. The mood allowed for something more than all-or-nothing solutions; limits on the possibility of action were admitted; there was more and more recognition that some issues were not capable of solution in the short run and that palliatives of temporary utility were all anybody could offer.

But not all segments of elite opinion shared in this passive, permissive frame of mind. The advent of African-Asian economically underdeveloped nations and the strident tone they lent to debate did not go unnoticed. The shift in power from the Security Council to the General Assembly was deplored by some people because it gave strength to "rampant nationalism, fuzzy and irresponsible resolutions, and the violation of domestic jurisdiction" [2] in the UN. The West was increasingly urged not to underwrite all UN operations while the Afro-Asian states indulged in "financial irresponsibility" by voting for large programs and then refusing to pay for them. The Afro-Asian states were asked to "grow up" politically. Some kind of weighted voting formula was suggested to compensate the West for the numerical preponderance of new and small nations in the Assembly. Most important, the government was asked not to use the UN as a substitute for national policy, to continue to seek the attainment of American objectives outside the UN as well as in.

A subtle combination of perceptions accounts for this critical stance. Domestic unrest in the United States increasingly involved the twin themes of race relations and equality; international unrest seemed to follow a similar pattern. In domestic relations, the volume of the dissenting and reforming voices seemed proportional to the enactment of concessions in the form of the civil rights and antipoverty programs; in the General Assembly the non-Western dissenters and reformers, apparently, could do no wrong. When they claimed territory by force (India in Goa, Indonesia against Malaya), the UN took no action; when they intervened in the domestic politics of their neighbors (in the Congo, South Africa, Angola, Rhodesia) the protection of human rights took precedence over the rule against intervention. Subversion, outside support for subversives, "indirect aggression," and race relations assumed the quality of a single syndrome of threat that seemed to link events in American ghettos to conditions in Africa. Conditions that would otherwise seem remote became a source of considerable malaise. There was, therefore, considerable opposition to the UN's role in the Congo, because it was played to support some foes of Western influence. Since neither Rhodesia nor South Africa directly threatened world peace with their restrictive racial policies some Americans could not see why they should be condemned as aggressors simply to give satisfaction to the new African nations. In Latin America and Southeast Asia, where civil strife in many countries went hand in hand with externally supported Communist subversion, appeals to the United Nations on behalf of the rebels were sometimes seen by these critics as direct challenges to American interests.

The United States government at first reacted negatively to the new tone of militant nonalignment, even though it bowed to it in Korea. President Eisenhower and Secretary of State Dulles condemned as "immoral" any attempt at neutrality between democracy and communism. They de-

[2] Raymond A. Moore, ed., *The United Nations Reconsidered* (Columbia, S.C.: University of South Carolina, 1963), p. 11.

veloped the formula of "indirect aggression"—the Eisenhower Doctrine—whereby the United States assumed the right to come to the assistance of any government calling for help against civil strife aided by external forces. Since the UN was not convinced that such situations represent classic cases of aggression, the containment policy had to be implemented bilaterally. The Southeast Asia Treaty Organization and the Central Treaty Organization of the Middle East were created as a method of implementing the doctrine. Marines were landed in Lebanon as a more direct way of supporting a shaky government. President Kennedy followed the same course in Vietnam, and President Johnson in the Dominican Republic.

In the UN, however, the doctrine was not accepted, and the United States quickly learned that direct intervention can be dangerous and embarrassing unless it succeeds rapidly or commands general support. Hence in conflicts of a local nature, outside the Cold War entirely or to be kept outside it to prevent escalation, the United States soon proved amenable to a new type of UN action and a new consensual principle for launching it. The action originated in the 1956 Suez-Sinai war, and it featured UN peacekeeping forces, contributed entirely by small nations, with the mission to separate the combatants and to fight only in carrying out this mandate. Such forces have since been used also in Cyprus (1964–68), the Congo (1960–63), and West Irian (1962); their withdrawal from Sinai in 1967 triggered the Arab-Israeli war of that year. Although no American troops were ever used, the United States provided transportation and financial support, sometimes of crucial proportions. In the Congo, at any rate, the United States felt that the UN operation successfully stopped internal war as well, even though the pro-American influence of the UN was stressed only by the "new Africa" section of the State Department (led by G. Mennen Williams) against the opposition of the "old Europe" wing.

"Permissive engagement," the consensual principle on which these operations rested, involves the Secretary-General rather than a single great power or a bloc of members as the initiator, organizer, and inspiration. But the UN membership must still "permit" the Secretary-General to "engage" the organization. Hence the procedures we identified as "balancing" and as the big power "concert" still remain appropriate as alternative ways through which an active Secretary-General can provide himself with a working majority. Balancing confirms dependence on the nonaligned; the concert obviates this but compels agreement with Moscow and Washington.

Because the other members of the UN—especially the nonaligned countries of Africa and Asia whom the United States desperately wished to keep out of the Communist orbit, whether Chinese or Russian—strenuously opposed intervention by the West, the United States learned to tolerate peacekeeping by the military forces of small countries as a way of protecting the national interest in local conflicts. This acceptance, however, brought with it two further consequences not clearly anticipated. First, operations of this kind cost a considerable amount, and few nations outside the West were anxious to pay for them. The Soviet Union and France objected to two such operations (Suez and the Congo) because they rested on "permissive engagement" and "balancing" rather than the Charter-inscribed concert. They declined to pay their shares. Second, because the procedure for passing peacekeeping resolutions demanded a strong Secretary-General or a two-thirds majority in the General Assembly, the special role of big powers seemed seriously threatened. How did the United States respond to these developments?

The prolonged financial crisis engendered by the dispute over peace-keeping and permissive engagement marks the high-water point of American commitment to collective security not controlled from Washington. The United States sought to rely on a decision of the International Court of Justice, which held that all UN members were *bound* to contribute to the expenses incurred in peacekeeping operations, whether they had voted for them or not. Had this decision become a law of international conduct, both permissive engagement and balancing would have become dominant; however, France, the Soviet Union, and many smaller nations opposed the American and the Court's position. By 1965 the United States had abandoned its position and admitted that future peacekeeping operations would have to depend heavily on *voluntary* contributions, primarily from industrial countries. Further, the Security Council rather than the General Assembly or the Secretary-General would once more be the legitimate source of action and consensus. In coming to this conclusion, Washington in effect came to agree with Moscow and Paris that emphasis should once more be shifted to the concert of the powers. And those who deplored excessive dependence on the votes of inexperienced Asian and African nations thus adapted to the multibloc world by resuscitating the Security Council, thereby seeking to escape the restraints of catering to the nonaligned.

By the mid-Sixties the United States had learned that the UN, no matter which system and which consensual formula prevails, is no substitute for national policy. But it also learned that because the UN was unable to end the Cold War, the mere winning of propaganda votes at Turtle Bay was no great boon. Instead, America had come to understand that UN action is able to neutralize trouble spots, prevent escalation, keep Cold War probes limited, and thus keep the Cold War from spreading. But the web of interdependence woven by these lessons is a frail one. An America determined to realize its vision abroad, in a Cold War setting, will not be enmeshed, as proved by Vietnam above all else. Direct confrontations between the big powers will be solved directly by them, not by the UN.

And so the lessons have been selective and the resulting rules full of loopholes. There has been a minimum of learning that results in institutionalization. At most, the United States has learned when *not* to use the UN as a tool of its policy and how to play the UN for its greatest effectiveness when it is used. The criterion of effectiveness, for the United States as for any other nation, remains the service rendered for advancing national objectives. The hallmark of political development for any human association may very well be the degree of "institutionalization" achieved by the collectivity. Institutionalization must mean more than stability and adaptation, for the UN's organs and procedures have been both stable and adaptive. It must mean more than mere growth in task and competence, for the UN has experienced steady growth. *Institutionalization must mean that the organs and their procedures become valued and accepted by the member nations as legitimate sources of policy even when that policy is not favored by the member.* In this sense, the United States has not revalued the UN for the maintenance of world peace. What can we hazard about the future?

THE UN AND THE FUTURE OF WORLD PEACE

It is most probable that the future will bring more local conflict, more border disputes among new nations, more civil strife supported from beyond a country's borders. It is equally probable that the great powers, especially the United States, will continue to be confronted with international radical and revolutionary movements unwilling to respect national sovereignty and official frontiers, particularly in Latin America and Southeast Asia. What would be the reaction of the American public to an increased peacekeeping task on the part of the UN in such a situation? How legitimate would the UN be as an institution if it were to interpose itself between the United States and its foreign antagonists?

Gallup Poll data accumulated in 1965 and 1966 suggests some answers. It is a striking fact that 59 per cent of Americans believe that the UN saved the world from another major war. Seventy-four per cent approved of a general move to ask the UN to try to work out *its own* formula for peace in Vietnam. And 62 per cent approved of a specific proposal involving UN-supervised elections, reciprocal troop withdrawals, and a standby American force offshore. However, when the public was asked pointedly whether the United States should abide by *any* UN decision regarding a solution in Vietnam, only 49 per cent were favorable.[3] It appears, therefore, that, as before, much blind faith continues to inhere in the UN *and* in Washington, thus bestowing considerable legitimacy on the procedures that flourish along the East River and the Potomac.

Elite opinion, however, does not match this picture entirely. While the major labor unions and business organizations follow the lead of the government in defending American moves, whether inside the UN or through external channels, many individual business and labor leaders do not. Many favor UN action on principle, even when in opposition to policy in Washington. Others tend to be more and more skeptical of international organizations not controlled by the West. Some say bluntly that if Communist China were admitted to the UN, the United States should leave the organization. Church leaders increasingly espouse internationalist positions perceived as conflicting with government policy, as do students and many professionals.

Congressional majorities, on the other hand, have been far more skeptical and reluctant to embrace the UN as a guarantor of American security. This became very apparent in 1962 when President Kennedy sought to persuade Congress to authorize the purchase of $100 million worth of UN bonds in order to finance peacekeeping operations. In fact, the financial crisis of the UN was in some measure the result of congressional insistence that other nations assume a heavier burden in financing UN military operations. Congress, by narrow committee majorities, approved a very restrictive measure authorizing the conditional purchase of bonds, linked to

[3] Gallup Polls, June 25, 1965; August, 1965; February 9, 1966; April 17, 1966.

the withholding of interest and amortization payments from the annual American contribution to the UN budget. Events since have done little to increase congressional respect for, and reliance on, UN security operations.

There is then considerable evidence that the earlier American consensus on the UN and American policy toward world peace, a consensus that blindly equated UN peacekeeping and enforcement with the American national interest, is about to break up. Contradictions between the two positions are becoming more apparent as the United States engages in military action not condoned by the world forum. They also become sharper as the organization intercedes in disputes in ways not considered acceptable by all sections of the American public. As the influence of the non-Western and economically underdeveloped members rises, some sections of the American public will become alienated from the UN; others will come to embrace it more passionately. Some people tend to argue in favor of more national initiatives and more multilateral ties, both economic and military, among the North Atlantic nations, and they tend to oppose American involvement in all military crises elsewhere—whether by way of intervention or in response to UN decisions. In short, the permissive and benevolent mood of the last twenty years is no longer to be taken for granted.

Nor can we rely on the continuity of the present system of blocs, even though neutralism has become respectable in the eyes of Washington. Instead of one nonaligned bloc of Africans and Asians, we will have an increasing trend toward bloc proliferation in the UN, involving committed Asians against nonaligned ones, pro-Western Africans as against neutral or pro-Communist ones, radical Latin Americans as against those favoring the United States. At the same time, these proliferating blocs tend to agree on less and less regarding the substance of world peace. The procedures of UN intercession, based on neutralist balancing between the major blocs and the creative initiatives of Secretary-General Dag Hammarskjöld, may be losing, rather than gaining, relevance here.

Yet both major political parties seem to advocate steps more appropriate to the past internationalist system than to the one we are entering. Republicans have been advocating the strengthening of the Secretary-General's capacity to mount peacekeeping forces, prepare military plans, and be ready to administer strife-torn new nations. They feel that the UN's financial independence ought to be strengthened and voting power should be made more proportional to the voting country's real strength. A high Republican group stated their position:

> Republicans take a realistic view of what the UN can and cannot do. We do not believe, as do some, that it is a panacea for the problems of the world; nor do we believe it works against our national interest. Experience has shown that the UN on many occasions has been useful in easing international tensions and in implementing our own foreign policy objectives.[4]

Democrats do not differ greatly in approach. They, too, favor strengthening UN military planning capacity and the Secretary-General (even though the Johnson Administration had less than complete confidence in the incum-

[4] Report of the Republican Coordinating Committee, meeting in Washington on June 27-28, 1966. *San Francisco Chronicle*, July 12, 1966.

ent, U Thant). They also favor the creation of additional national standby orces, capable of being turned into peacekeeping personnel at short notice. Although neither Democrats nor Republicans envisage any drastic institutional innovations approaching some species of world government, Democrats tend to favor increased powers for the International Court of Justice through repeal of the Connally Reservation. And in order to escape both the programmatic and financial "irresponsibility" of the General Assembly the Democratic Administration has favored a return to the pre-eminence of the Security Council in matters relating to world peace, a course it favors over the introduction of a weighted voting formula.[5]

Undoubtedly, the United States is more enmeshed in the web of interdependence now and for the future than was thought possible in 1945 or 1950. The consequences of the containment policy pursued in the United Nations were far from expected, and the lessons learned by American policymakers resulted in additional interdependence in the period that followed. The consequences that developed from decolonization likewise resulted in institutional accretions to the UN that had not been planned or even advocated by the United States. Yet the desire for peace and for the exclusion of the Soviet Union from Africa and Asia seemed to leave Washington little choice, unless it wished to intervene on its own. When it did intervene, the cry was loud enough to discourage a unilateral repetition of the episode, because it seemed to cost too many friends and render unneutral too many neutrals. Expediency alone dictates continued dependence on the web, and expediency alone supports policies designed to create standing, well-trained, easily transportable, nonfighting UN forces able to intercede in the minor squabbles outside the Cold War framework.

But bipolar nuclear deterrence will continue to be the tamer of the Cold War itself, not the UN. And as nuclear weapons become more and more widely accessible, the role of the UN in keeping the peace may be called into question. If, at the same time, peacekeeping and enforcement will increasingly take place at the expense of the West and only in the service of the UN majority, the desire to break the fragile bonds of the web may become irresistible in the United States. Hence we must round out our analysis of national and collective security by examining the UN's efforts to tame the nuclear threat. Perhaps disarmament can finally enmesh nation and world, to protect both.

THE PROTECTING WING OR THE UNIVERSAL EMBRACE?
DISARMAMENT NEGOTIATIONS UNTIL 1958

The large powers have been engaging in disarmament negotiations almost continuously since 1921, interrupted only by major wars among them. These negotiations have overwhelmingly failed to achieve the objective of making the world secure. Why? Chief Soviet negotiator Maxim Litvinov taunted the West in 1932 by asking, "Why don't you just abolish

---

[5] For views of the Johnson Administration see Richard N. Gardner, *In Pursuit of World Order* (New York: Frederick A. Praeger, Inc., 1964), pp. 94 ff.

your armies and navies if you are serious about establishing peace?" To which Salvador de Madariaga replied:

> The animals decided to disarm, and held a Conference for that purpose. The eagle, with an eye on the bull, suggested that all horns should be razed off. The bull, with a squint at the tiger, thought that all claws should be cut short. The tiger, glaring at the elephant, was of the opinion that tusks should be pulled out or at any rate shortened. The elephant, staring at the eagle, thought it indispensable that all wings should be clipped. Whereupon the bear, with a circular glance at all his brethren, cried out: "Why all those half-way measures? Let all weapons be done away with, so that nothing remains in the way of a fraternal, all-embracing hug." [6]

Clearly, then, collective security and disarmament are closely related. Total disarmament involves complete mutual trust. To abolish national arms implies a willingness to secure peace by way of international police forces, that is, enough confidence in the UN to delegate peacekeeping to someone else's soldiers. Completely successful collective security is inconceivable without significant disarmament; disarmament is inconceivable without mutual trust. Since the bipolar and multipolar systems have not been characterized by large quantities of confidence and good faith among nations, the failure of disarmament is easily explained. Yet this is too simple an answer because it does not explain why the negotiations nevertheless continue and what, if anything, the parties learn from them. Nor does the failure of complete disarmament explain when and how more limited steps, wholly compatible with improved collective security, can be insinuated into the international system.

Basically, the policy of the United States after the end of World War II was to pursue negotiations that would disarm the Soviet Union while leaving intact the American superiority in nuclear weapons. The Soviet Union's policy, not irrationally, was the mirror image of America's. To disarm, then, meant to disarm your enemy. It would be useless and tiresome to set forth, even in summary form, the many disarmament proposals advanced in the various UN committees. None were approved prior to 1958. All foundered because the United States insisted on four features that the Soviet Union interpreted as perpetuating American arms superiority: (1) Disarmament was presented as a *package* of interconnected items of a symmetrical nature, a uniform percentage reduction in ground forces to be accompanied by a uniform reduction in uranium processing capacity or bomber strength. The right package to satisfy both sides was never found. (2) *Inspection* of remaining arms was demanded and the United States proposed a large and well-equipped force of inspectors. The Soviets sometimes argued that the United States was more interested in inspection than in disarmament. (3) Disarmament was divided into fixed *stages* designed to perpetuate whatever technological advantages the United States enjoyed at the time a proposal was advanced, and the success of the inspection was specified as a precondition for advancing to the next stage. (4) The United States insisted on foolproof *control* over the results of inspections; punitive

---

[6] Salvador de Madariaga, *The Burning of the Parthenon* (New York: Frederick A. Praeger, 1960), p. 70.

ction without the possibility of a veto was to be taken forthwith against a violator of the rules. Invariably the United States insisted that arms were not so much a cause of tension and insecurity as a symptom of distrust and latent aggression. Once the Cold War abated and every nation abided by the rules of the Charter, meaningful arms limitation could be discussed.

Sometimes the proposals linked disarmament with intelligence gathering or improving possibly unreliable weapons systems. Without an efficient radar warning system, the first generation of soft missiles, for example, were of dubious reliability. President Eisenhower proposed the "open sky" plan (1955) as a way to prevent surprise attacks and gather intelligence. He also advanced the "Atoms for Peace" plan (1953), the sole proposal that bore fruit at this time. That scheme resulted in the creation of the International Atomic Energy Agency (IAEA) in 1957. It sought to combine the interests of underdeveloped countries in gaining nuclear lore and access to peaceful nuclear power with the interests of the major powers in preventing nuclear proliferation. Toward that end it was decided that fissionable materials made available for peaceful purposes should not be diverted to military use, and an international inspection service was set up under IAEA to control nondiversion. By appealing to an economic motive, therefore, the United States took a roundabout step in legitimating an international inspection service previously rejected by the Soviet Union.

Did the American public back the government's policy of putting national security ahead of collective security? By and large it did. Far from being compelled to change its policy as a result of public clamor or because of popular fear of nuclear fallout, opinion seemed to shift in response to autonomously determined changes in government policy. Between 1946 and 1953, approval of international control of atomic energy varied between 31 per cent and 61 per cent of the public, and this at a time when government policy favored such a scheme, subject to the conditions listed above. When, during the mid-Fifties, the government stressed the importance of nuclear weapons and the allegedly limited health hazard posed by atmospheric testing, most of the public went along; when the government reversed its arguments in 1958, however, most of the public fell into line again. The more highly educated tended to favor the suspension of tests and feared the hazards of fallout. Party became a salient predictor of attitudes only during the election of 1956, when the Democrats' Adlai Stevenson came out in favor of a test ban and President Eisenhower opposed it. When the government vacillated thereafter between unilateral cessations and resumptions of tests, the public once more followed, only to approve the limited test ban treaty, once it was concluded.

American scientists, the segment of the elite most emotionally and professionally involved with the issue, also divided into several groups. Their views were significant because the technical naïveté of many political leaders compelled attention to the scientific community's arguments and because most of the actual disarmament and arms control proposals advanced by the United States actually originated with scientists. Some scientists felt that international control, though desirable, was possible only with full world government. Since this was held unattainable, a continued national policy of nuclear superiority was strongly advocated. Others, while

agreeing that containment was necessary, also argued that a danger po
is reached in bipolar confrontations that has to be met with appropria
curbs on arms; and it is this school that ultimately gained control of the Stat
Department's Arms Control Agency. Finally, the most vociferous and active
group equates the arms race with vestigial human irrationality, as per-
sonified by political and military leaders, and holds out for unilateral disarmament as the only way to unwind the vicious spiral of arms, distrust,
more arms, and more distrust, with nuclear war the inevitable outcome.
The impact of this group of scientists on the peace movement has been
overwhelming, merged as it is with arguments against war drawn from
mental health, psychiatry, and pacifism, but its influence on the public and
on policy remains marginal.

What, then, caused the government to alter its disarmament policy
that sought to disarm the Soviet Union first? Certainly it was not any
dramatic shift in public opinion among the mass of citizens. But there did
develop in elite circles an awareness that the direct and total approach to
disarmament had been utterly futile, while the dangers of nuclear war kept
rising. Few would agree with astronomer Harlow Shapley when he contrasted the idealistic scientist with the do-nothing diplomat:

> All goes smoothly. We in the International Geophysical Year [a major inter-
> national cooperative venture in many branches of science] cooperate; in
> the UN they expostulate. . . . I pause here a second to exclaim, uselessly,
> "curses on the diplomats." Useless—but it gives me a bit of relief.[7]

But others, from 1958 on, began seriously to consider partial and separate
steps toward arms limitation rather than massive package deals, in the hope
of first steps leading to cumulative, later strides. An agreement to suspend
the testing of nuclear weapons was high on the list of first steps. President
Eisenhower's offer to the Soviet Union to negotiate a separate test ban
treaty was suggested by Secretary of State Dulles, not by the scientists.
What had caused the change in position?

Two major developments in the international system itself, not at
home, proved to be the causes. One was the pressure of small and nonaligned nations in the increasingly multipolar world of 1958. Previous
negotiations had taken place in the Security Council, the General Assembly
and in special meetings convoked or sanctioned by the UN. After 1958, the
pattern became one of separate negotiations *in secret* among the major
powers, encouraged by the UN and conducted under its auspices. The most
recent formula is that of the Eighteen Nation Disarmament Committee
(ENDC), made up of five Western, five Communist, and eight nonaligned
nations, with the nonaligned acting as mediators between the major blocs.
The formula symbolizes the response of the international system to the
threat of arms; it also illustrates the increasing responsiveness of the United
States to this concern.

More important, however, is the threat of weapons itself. No longer
a symptom of tensions, the hyperweapons of our era were increasingly perceived by policy-makers as a major cause of tensions, particularly as the

---

[7] Quoted in Douglas Hurd, "A Case for the Diplomats," *Bulletin of the Atomic
Scientists*, 16, No. 2 (February, 1960), 52.

Soviet Union matched every American technological advance. Secretary of State Herter clearly articulated the motivation behind this new mood:

> We approach these new negotiations with some hope that the Soviet leaders may be coming to realize that the arms race offers unacceptable risks. This realization could induce them to attach a higher priority to progress in arms control, as being in their own national interest.[8]

Herter went on to point out major dangers associated with an uncontrolled arms race. Proliferation could put nuclear weapons in the hands of irresponsible governments, and present strategic missile systems had such a short reaction time that a war by miscalculation was quite possible. These dangers should be met by agreements that would safeguard against surprise attack, allow exchange of information in times of crisis to assure an opponent that nuclear attack was not planned, and ban nuclear testing for the purpose of halting the increasing probability of proliferation.

President Eisenhower made clear that he feared catastrophe for both nations because of their weapons, and U.S. negotiator Wadsworth argued very cogently that, for the first time, it was the character of the weapons technology itself that caused the United States to change its policy:

> The expanding pace of technological developments can result in unpredictable and erratic breakthroughs, and shifts in the precarious military balance could induce an aggressor to wage war when possessed of a temporary advantage.[9]

> Ours is a world of growing dangers. There is a danger of surprise attack prepared in secret. There is the danger of nuclear attack from outer space. There is the menace of constantly mounting stockpiles of nuclear weapons and large armies. There is the peril of spreading capability for the production of modern weapons to greater numbers of Nations. There is the hazard of war by accident or miscalculation. We hold that these dangers must be dealt with now.[10]

This approach was accepted by President Kennedy, who shared his predecessor's belief in the possibility of limited arms control agreements as a slow curtain raiser for a comprehensive agreement. He also shared his predecessor's concern that it was the character of the arms race itself that produced the danger. Because both the United States and the Soviet Union had reached heights of invulnerability, they could both afford to cut back. The experience of the Cuban missile crisis must have contributed greatly to this mood. Pending the creation of a genuine collective security system with a UN Peace Force, then, the cumulative defusing of the nuclear world remained the American position in and out of the UN. "We believe that disarmament in balanced steps would increase the security of the whole world, including ourselves," said Dean Rusk.[11]

---

[8] U.S. Department of State, *Documents on Disarmament, 1960*, p. 46.

[9] *Ibid.*, p. 312.

[10] *Ibid.*, p. 324.

[11] "Disarmament and Arms Control," *Department of State Bulletin* (July 2, 1962), p. 7.

ARMS CONTROL AND THE FUTURE OF COLLECTIVE SECURITY

Since that time, the United States and the Soviet Union have installed the "hot line" communications link between Moscow and Washington (1963), and have agreed on four major arms control steps that also require implementation on the part of other countries. The partial test ban (1963) is one step, though France and China have failed to adhere to the treaty. The outlawry of nuclear weapons in space and the non-annexation of celestial bodies, an agreement concluded under UN auspices (1966), is another major step. A similar agreement was concluded in 1959 for Antarctica, at the same time throwing it open to the inspection of any party to the treaty. Finally, the superpowers achieved agreement on a nuclear nonproliferation treaty (1968) that prevents them from aiding non-nuclear nations in the development of nuclear weapons and "other nuclear explosive devices." The IAEA was given new inspection powers under the pact to assure that the non-nuclears divert none of their fissionable materials to such purposes. But since some key countries have so far declined to adhere to the text, the scope of IAEA inspections remains unclear.

Significantly, these negotiations have pitted the nuclear powers against non-nuclear ones, quite irrespective of alliance and ideological links. Some non-nuclears increasingly fear that a nonproliferation pact would deprive them of access to nuclear technology and hinder their industrial development; therefore the draft treaty assures them that the nuclear powers will support a special aid program to avoid this possibility and guarantee the sharing of all in peaceful nuclear experiments. Others feel that unless the nuclear powers also considerably cut back their level of arms, foregoing the acquisition of nuclear weapons would condemn nations such as Japan, India, and West Germany to indefinite inferiority. And in the absence of nuclear arms, how would they protect themselves against possible nuclear blackmail by states not party to the treaty?

Concurrently with the acceptance of the treaty draft, the General Assembly demanded that immediate progress be made toward complete nuclear and general disarmament, a demand to which the superpowers began to accede in 1968. Discussions were also launched, aiming at completing the Partial Test Ban Treaty by including underground explosions. But while Britain and the United States continued to argue for the need of international on-site inspection, the Soviet Union reiterated that the ban could be self-enforcing because of adequate detection equipment in the possession of each superpower. To reassure non-nuclear nations against the possibility of blackmail before all these developments are culminated in new agreements and institutions, the Security Council adopted a resolution recognizing that nuclear aggression would have to be met with an immediate response from the superpowers. Acting under the Charter's article authorizing unilateral acts of self-defense, the major powers have a free hand to extend their protective nuclear umbrella over fearful non-nuclear nations. The UN therefore endorsed the Soviet-American declaration of aid to victims of nuclear threats from nonsignatories. This endorsement, however, contributes little to making the guarantee very credible, since the superpowers retain full freedom of action; conversely, each could veto an explicit Security Council resolution ordering the execution of nuclear guarantees.

Arms control, however, did not mean that efforts at comprehensive disarmament were given up. Like the Soviet Union, the United States committed itself to this goal and, like the Russians, submitted a comprehensive scheme to ENDC. Table 6 (pp. 52–53) contrasts the two schemes and makes plain how much closer to a consensus the international system has propelled the superpowers since the earlier days, when disarmament negotiations were little more than Cold War propaganda battles. Note particularly the American insistence on the creation of a UN Peace Force as the crucial step in Stage 3.

Public opinion did not speak with any uniform voice during this period either. In 1960 and in 1963 the public, in almost equal proportions, supported and opposed UN-supervised multilateral arms reduction. Sixty-three per cent of the public supported ratification of the test ban treaty in 1963; 79 per cent thought in 1961 that Khrushchev was bluffing when he supported the same treaty.[12] Nor did elites present a uniform position. Study groups and task forces in both political parties supported the continuation of arms control steps. While fearful that disarmament, and to a lesser extent even arms control, would mean a decline in business, some segments of American industry nevertheless began to study the kind of change-over that a reduction in the arms budget would imply. In cooperation with the Arms Control Agency studies were made to find out how the electronic industry could contribute to the manufacture of new detection systems. A few labor unions took the same adaptive position, but many ignored the issue. While some spokesmen for the military and for business deplored the outlawry of space weapons and of testing, the bulk of the American elite once more responded to the policy initiatives of Washington. Many business leaders welcomed the cut in taxes and the promise of greater stability and predictability of world conditions if disarmament were to progress.

The major challenge to this line of thought came from the peace groups dedicated to unilateral steps toward disarmament. They actually feared the progress of arms control measures because these tend to stabilize, not abolish, the balance of terror and the deterrent system. To the unilateralist, only schemes that would clearly lead to the abolition of arms through some graduated program of mutual reduction initiated by the United States were morally acceptable. Hence the efforts of the Arms Control Agency were attacked by this segment of the public because they did not go far enough but confirmed the *status quo*.

Controlling arms in one part of the globe need not be a reason to curtail waging war elsewhere. Unilateralists feared this, and President Johnson demonstrated it as he escalated hostile measures in Vietnam while unilaterally reducing the production of enriched uranium and shutting down some plutonium piles. At the same time, he called for more cession of peaceful fissionable material to the IAEA and voluntarily strengthened the

[12] Gallup Polls, November 23, 1960; November 26, 1961; November 29, 1961; September 1, 1963; September 18, 1963.

TABLE 6 · DISARMAMENT PROPOSALS (AS OF 1966) USSR-USA

Topics	Stage 1	Stage 2	Stage 3
Duration			
USSR	18 months.	24 months.	12 months.
USA	36 months.	36 months.	"as promptly as possible."
Nuclear weapons			
USSR	Cease testing and outlaw transfers of weapons.	Eliminate all weapons of mass destruction.	Eliminate all weapons of mass destruction.
USA	Cease testing under international control and outlaw transfers of weapons.	Reduce nuclear weapons to minimum levels.	
Delivery systems			
USSR	Eliminate all delivery systems (except small number of homebased ICBM's).		Eliminate all delivery systems.
USA	Reduce delivery systems by 30%.	Reduce delivery systems by additional 50%.	Eliminate all delivery systems.
Outer space			
USSR	Prohibit all military uses of space.		
USA	Refrain from orbiting nuclear weapons and limit production, stockpiling, and boosters for space vehicles.		
Conventional arms			
USSR	Reduce by 30%.	Reduce by an additional 35%.	Eliminate except as required for internal peacekeeping.
USA	Reduce by 30%.	Reduce by an additional 50%.	Eliminate except as required for internal peacekeeping.
Military manpower			
USSR	Reduce American and Soviet armies to 1.9 million men each.	Reduce both armies to 1 million men.	Reduce to number necessary to maintain domestic order and provide contingents for UN police force.
USA	Reduce Soviet and American armies to 2.1 million men each.	Reduce both armies by 50%.	

Military budgets			
USSR	Reduce military budgets proportionately to arms and manpower reductions.		
USA	Submit reports on military budgets and seek agreement on verifiable reductions.		Limit military expenditures to maintaining international and national police forces.
Military bases			
USSR	Eliminate foreign bases and withdraw all troops.		
USA		Eliminate specific foreign bases through agreement.	Eliminate foreign bases and withdraw all troops.
Transitional measures			
USSR	Prohibit joint, and require advance notice of national, military movements and maneuvers; exchange military missions; establish communications systems.		
USA	Give advance notice of major military movements; exchange military missions; establish observation posts and communications systems.		
Inspection and peacekeeping			
USSR	Establish IDO* to supervise destruction of arms. IDO to function under Security Council.	IDO supervision of arms destruction.	Place national militia contingents under Security Council direction; command of troop units vested in body composed of "three principal groups of states" and each must agree to peacekeeping actions.
USA	Establish IDO to inspect and control destroyed and remaining arms. IDO to function under Security Council.	IDO inspection and control over disarmament steps and remaining arms.	UN Peace Force to function under Security Council; veto power not applicable to peacekeeping actions.

* International Disarmament Organization.

Source: Jack C. Plano and Robert E. Riggs, *Forging World Order* (New York: Macmillan, 1967), pp. 333-34.

inspection power of that UN agency by placing certain national America installations, as well as bilateral reactor programs, under its jurisdiction. Yet, simultaneously, he also intensified the arms race by committing the United States to the creation of a Manned Orbital Laboratory, to more surveillance satellites overflying enemy countries, and to an Anti-Ballistic Missile System. In the summer of 1968, these steps were countered with joint American-Soviet proposals to ENDC to forbid the placement of weapons on the ocean floor and the seabed. Further, the two governments informed ENDC that they expect to begin bilateral negotiations aiming at the reciprocal limitation of offensive strategic nuclear weapons delivery systems, as well as defenses against ballistic missiles. Yet these negotiations were delayed by the Soviet invasion of Czechoslovakia. In short, it is unclear how enmeshed is the United States in arms control arrangements. Nor is it clear how seriously one can take the official policy of trusting a UN Peace Force as the sole agency for maintaining collective security after the advent of complete disarmament.

American enmeshment into the frail web of UN organs, agencies, and committees is minimal. Arms control arrangements are mostly self-enforcing, and the inspection powers of the IAEA remain to be tested. UN influence manifests itself primarily in the verbal and moral pressure exercised by the smaller nonaligned nations. For example, the World Health Organization continues to pass resolutions demanding that resources made available by cutting defense budgets be transferred to development aid projects. Very similar resolutions have been adopted by other UN agencies. When the UN Conference on Trade and Development did so, the United States was the sole nation to vote "no" while the Soviet Union abstained. Yet, the United States began to bow to this pressure in 1968 when it announced that strong measures must soon be taken under the new Non-Proliferation Treaty, to assure the non-nuclear nations of the benefits of the peaceful use of atomic energy; toward that end it was proposed that IAEA be used to conduct peaceful nuclear explosions and intensify its nuclear technical aid.

The General Assembly is often used as a forum for the discussion of nuclear-free zones, world agreements banning the introduction of nuclear weapons into areas such as Africa and Latin America. After some hesitation, the United States came to favor the arrangement for Latin America. A text banning the testing, use, manufacture, production, acquisition, and possession of any nuclear weapon on the territory of any signatory was adopted in 1967 and ratified by some Latin-American nations during 1968. Its effectiveness, however, also remains in doubt because, of the nuclear nations, only the United States has given the guarantees of compliance that the treaty expects of all. Furthermore, European nations with territories in the Western Hemisphere have so far declined to give assurances that they will observe the ban in their Caribbean possessions. Finally, the treaty does not ban "peaceful" nuclear explosions, a situation creating uneasiness among the nuclear powers because of their certainty that there is little technical difference between "peaceful" and "weapons-related" blasts.

On the other hand, NATO powers rejected numerous proposals for the creation of inspected nuclear-free zones in Central Europe, because they would tend to strengthen the Warsaw Pact forces disproportionately. Sug-

....ions for regional arms control arrangements of other kinds continue to made, and many may become attractive to groups of states as they ach a military equilibrium that satisfies everyone, so that armaments can be cut back without disproportionate losses of national security. Agreements among industrial nations not to sell arms to Africa or the Middle East rank high among such suggestions. Others involve bilateral agreements on mutual inspection, such as a Soviet-American mutual surveillance pact for the Arctic. The pursuit of such steps, of course, would doom further the already marginal position of the advocates of dramatic unilateral disarmament.

The future relationship between disarmament and collective security is most ambiguous. Consider this argument: the possession of nuclear weapons enables a nation to play a role far beyond the limits imposed by size, population and tradition. Nuclear weapons may be the great equalizer of world politics. This lesson was learned first by the possessors of these weapons, the superpowers. Test bans and nonproliferation agreements, apart from making the globe a safer place for us all, also tend to perpetuate the extraordinary power of the United States and the Soviet Union. And this fact may doom them if nations such as India, Israel, Egypt or Indonesia prove unwilling in the future to accept collective security arrangements imposed on them by a concert in the Security Council and seek the possibility of independent action by way of national nuclear weapons. As the Middle Eastern war of 1967 showed, superpowers that successfully deter each other are immobilized if they also fear escalation from conventional war, thus giving a determined small nation considerable room for independent warlike maneuver. The UN has been quite unable to prevent this trend, and the proliferation of nuclear weapons would exacerbate it.

But now consider the opposite argument: escalating mutual fear will increasingly predispose the nations to accept the General and Complete Disarmament plans now in the hands of ENDC. The success of these plans, however, implies world government, because the agency that controls the UN Peace Force would, in effect, have to be responsible for world law and order. Complete disarmament implies world government, whether by the UN or some successor body, much as the implementation of the Baruch Plan for the internationalization of atomic energy would have spawned it in 1946. But do the nations want world government? There is not the slightest evidence that preponderant elites *anywhere* desire such a system, and many actively oppose it. Hence the failure of arms control to change the system could lead either indirectly and unwittingly to world government, or directly to the confirmation of the present system of imperfect collective security.

And this is perhaps the strongest argument outlining the future. In 1965 a special White House Conference on International Cooperation advised President Johnson to intensify his search for peace by way of various efforts to achieve disarmament. But the list of suggestions contains merely separate arms control items making up "further steps" leading—perhaps— toward general disarmament. Certainly the unilateralist flavor and passion is lacking.[13] In the meantime, the task of preserving world peace, however

[13] Richard N. Gardner, ed., *Blueprint for Peace* (New York: McGraw-Hill, 1966), pp. 48-51.

imperfectly, has once again become the primary responsibility of the
Security Council, the forum par excellence of the major powers.
decades were spent in efforts to outflank this system by means of regio
alliances, by the forum of mankind represented in the General Assemb.
through unilateral policies, propagandistic and grandiose disarmamer.
schemes, and limited arms control measures that reaffirm the thermonuclea
balance. But the inferences that the major powers unwillingly drew from
their own outflanking maneuvers persuaded them to reaffirm their enmeshment in the imperfections of the concert and the balancing process in the
Security Council. And so it will be as long as there is no massive nuclear
proliferation or general and complete disarmament. But what if there is
proliferation without the caution born from fear and knowledge of thermonuclear missilery, and what if this proliferation goes hand in hand with a
greater multiplicity of blocs, each seeking its own nuclear umbrella? No
known formula of national or collective security will be of much comfort
then.

4

World Economic Development, Trade, and Finance

Cotton marketing agreements, the flow of gold, and haggling over tariffs make less spectacular news than nuclear bomb tests, truce violations, or the disintegration of alliances; so do technical assistance, soft loans, and regional development doctrines. But they cause no less controversy, and they may entail human suffering and deprivation on a massive scale if they are not handled with care and solicitude. The practices of collective and selective security are tied to the ideological passions and fears of peoples and their leaders; but the practices of world trade, finance, and aid are as firmly rooted in convictions and commitments on what constitutes the good life and the good society—nationally as well as internationally. Mutually opposing values in the international trade and monetary arena, in and out of the United Nations, engender conflicts and patterns of accommodation that may enmesh the nation-state in its pursuit of welfare. The United States, a giant among world traders and investors, believes in free private enterprise, private capital, and competitive trading based on the liberal economist's doctrine of comparative advantage. Can it prevail in a world that does not share these values very consistently? More than twenty years of experience in the web of international organizational discussion suggest that it cannot.

THE FREE ENTERPRISE VISION
OF THE INTERNATIONAL ECONOMY

American policy-makers emerged from the cataclysm of World War II with well-articulated beliefs concerning the kind of economy they wanted for the peaceful and prosperous world that was expected to emerge from

the fighting. They wanted a world in which the economic cutthroat pract.
of the Great Depression of the 1930's would not be repeated. They a
wanted a world that would give scope to American private industry ar
agriculture, to sell abroad without suffering from tariff and quota dis
crimination or being victimized by unstable exchange rates and arbitrary
currency devaluation. Finally, they wanted the needs of capital-importing
nations to be served by American private investors rather than by government loans. In short, what they desired was a self-regulating, stable world
economy that would give scope to American enterprise and would require
a minimum of institutional control. The economic development of the less
wealthy nations and those devastated by the war would be advanced primarily through expanding world trade and private investment—not through
government-to-government assistance.

These beliefs were widely shared among the business elite and the
government. Economic issues are predominantly the preserve of the elites
who are able to identify their own interests in a global setting. There is no
articulate public opinion in the realm of trade and finance, as shown by the
unvarying pattern of equally divided positive, negative, and "don't know"
answers in public opinion polls on world economic questions. Only on
foreign aid does the mass public have opinions, vague and unstructured as
they are. In this chapter, therefore, we will be concerned largely with
interest group and governmental opinions and their evolution. It is of the
greatest importance to note the special ties that exist between certain interest
groups and agencies in Washington that relate directly to their demands
and needs. Economic policy-making is less consistently dominated by the
President than are military and security matters. The large departments of
the government speak with many, often conflicting voices and thus reflect
the aspirations of the elite groups that enjoy their confidence.

This was as true in 1945 as it is today. The Treasury Department and
the banking world identify with the essentially conservative attitudes out-
lined above and attempt their implementation through the International
Monetary Fund (IMF) and the International Bank for Reconstruction and
Development (IBRD), institutions set up largely in response to desires of
the financial community after World War II. American farmers, always
eager to sell their surpluses and maintain high agricultural prices, channel
their demands into the Department of Agriculture, which in turn seeks to
shape international policy by turning to the Food and Agriculture Organization (FAO) of the UN. American labor approaches world economic problems partly by preaching the need for free unions everywhere, higher skills,
manpower training, and productivity programs; it does so through the Department of Labor and the International Labor Organization (ILO). The
social welfare profession, charitable groups, women's organizations, teach-
ers, and communications specialists channel their demands for international
welfare services and relief organizations through the Department of Health,
Education, and Welfare, which is an important participant in the United
Nations Educational, Scientific and Cultural Organization (UNESCO), the
World Health Organization (WHO), and in special UN aid bodies such as
the UN Children's Fund. Most business groups channel their demands

ough the Department of Commerce; this agency, in turn, is an important aper of American foreign trade policy in the General Agreement on Tariffs id Trade (GATT) and in some regional organizations. And the Department of State? State is involved in all of these; but American representation in this tangle of international organizations is shared with the other departments, leaving State unable clearly and unambiguously to "plan" American economic policy. That policy, then, is the result of clashing and conflicting group interests and values reflected in equally discordant champions in Congress and in the Executive. Yet they all "make policy" when the President exerts no effort to pre-empt the field.

The postwar government approach to world economic problems has thus been shaped largely by business and banking interests. Neither of these groups, however, is internally homogeneous. One segment is "fundamentalist" in belief; it stands for the universal validity of the American Way of Life in free private enterprise, and it distrusts government regulation at the national or international level. Another, generally more powerful segment accepts these tenets but is ready in practice to adjust them to meet external obstacles. Further, and more importantly, this more powerful segment—usually found in the banks and big corporations on the northeastern and Pacific seaboards—is often ready to subordinate economic ideology to political imperatives. Thus, while spokesmen for this group advocated and endorsed the free enterprise approach to world economic entanglements in 1945, they were also prepared to sacrifice aspects of their ideological purity when Europe's failure to recover immediately called for the extraordinary *public* aid program we know as the Marshall Plan. Thinking in the Treasury Department differed from the business ethic only in that it added one Keynesian consideration: domestic prosperity was thought to depend on the international economy's taking up the slack of a recession at home without at the same time reintroducing the beggar-my-neighbor policies that had flourished during earlier depressions. Hence modest international pump priming through the IMF and the IBRD was seen as an ancillary device for assuring American prosperity.

The American master plan for a better world was made up of three interdependent parts relating to trade, money, and development, each the subject of prolonged international negotiations between 1944 and 1947. The UN had no prominent place in the plan. The basic ground rules of world trade were laid down in the Havana Charter and were to be administered by an autonomous International Trade Organization (ITO), a specialized agency-to-be of the UN. These rules governed permissible restrictions on private investment, dumping, trade in agricultural commodities and the prices to be fixed therefor, the permissibility of exchange controls and quotas on imports. Further, the charter laid down a basic rule: tariffs that discriminate by giving preferential treatment to certain countries—the British Commonwealth system was in everybody's mind—were to be eliminated by the consistent application of the most-favored-nation clause in international tariff bargaining. State trading was permitted but subject to special rules. The United States insisted on ITO rules and powers of regulation that would combat the economic nationalism of others, thus permitting American exports and investments to penetrate their protected and discriminatory tradi. systems. America had come of age and felt able to compete successfully wit all comers.

The second component of the master plan was the world monetary system, as institutionalized in the IMF. The essence of the system was stable exchange rates set authoritatively by an international agency in order to bar unilateral and arbitrary national devaluation of currencies, and the abolition of exchange controls, to free international capital movements. These objectives were to be accomplished by creating a world reserve of hard currencies—essentially dollars and sterling—and gold held by the IMF. When a country was tempted to change the value of its currency to cope with balance-of-payments difficulties, the IMF would give short-term assistance with hard currencies. About $9 billion in reserves was available. Changes in par values of currency beyond a fixed limit and not authorized by the IMF were illegal and could deprive the violating state of the right to draw on the IMF reserve in case of need.

On paper at least, the IMF was a powerful supranational organization. In reality, its institutional web masked American predominance in a world of soft currencies and IMF quotas very much smaller than the American share; for members' votes were weighted by their contributions of hard currency, and the dominant dollar augmented by America's large contribution made IMF an American institution.

America's favorite UN instrument of action, however, was the IBRD. There, the United States wielded 32 per cent of the voting power, compared to 25 per cent in the IMF. But votes were never taken in the IBRD, because the bank's successive presidents (all American) enjoyed the full confidence of major member nations and of the U.S. Treasury. Paul G. Hoffman, head of the UN Development Program and former administrator of the Marshall Plan, innocently described the close ties between Washington and IBRD:

> . . . we had no problem [in coordinating IBRD loan policy to the Marshall Plan] because we discussed all these loans they were thinking of making and they were always good enough to come to us and say, "What about the impact of this loan to Turkey? Do you think we ought to go ahead with it?" That was informal, and that is one of the best ways of control. . . .[1]

Successive high American officials and congressional leaders completely relied upon Eugene Black, the bank's powerful president from 1949 to 1962, to remain true to the more conservative aspects of the American approach to world economic problems. That approach, inspired by a vision of free enterprise, had definite consequences with respect to unwanted and as yet undigested acceptance of foreign aid. It implied a marked preference for private over public funds, "sound" finance over inflation, loans over gifts and outrights grants, bilateral operations over UN-sponsored activities that would imply sharing control with the recipient nations en bloc. Whether Black actually adhered to the conservative lines is part of the story of the major lesson learned by the United States.

[1] Quoted in I. L. Claude, *Swords Into Plowshares*, 3rd ed. (New York: Random House, 1964), p. 364.

THE WORLD ECONOMY AND THE TARNISHED VISION

America's economic ideology encountered three types of obstacles that prevented its victory; two of them resulted from events and attitudes outside the United States, but one was the result of internal pressures. Economic liberalism is rarely espoused with passion by economic groups that consider themselves high-cost producers unable to compete with rival imports, and American businessmen and farmers are no exception. The internal political environment, therefore, militated against a consistent policy of cutting tariffs for items produced at high cost in the United States. Further, it militated against a managed international commodity policy that would keep American farmers from selling their huge output at nationally subsidized prices; nor would it permit American importers of primary commodities to pay higher prices than the world market created.

The outside world posed a series of purely economic obstacles. The countries of Western Europe were not prepared to establish free trade or forego exchange controls or quotas as long as they thought a planned economy was required for postwar reconstruction. The underdeveloped countries were not yet in a position to make their views prevail, but they evinced no great enthusiasm for nondiscriminatory tariff rules that would subordinate their infant industries to powerful industrial exporters; nor were they eager for currency convertibility that would soon strain their balance of payments and limit their ability to devalue. Further, they wanted the power to resort to state trading and to regulate international commodity trade in order to stabilize the prices of primary products. The Soviet bloc, finally, branded the world trade system favored by the United States as the global version of exploitive capitalist imperialism and insisted on the central role of state trading and national protection *against* private investment. The Soviets therefore declined to join the IMF and the IBRD.

Perhaps the sharpest challenge to the free enterprise vision came from the external political force posed by the evolving Cold War. As the advance of communism in Europe came to be perceived as the major threat to the United States, Washington reacted by creating the largest and most successful foreign aid program ever devised. The program, among other things, also substituted grants for loans, soft loans for hard ones, permitted exchange controls and tariff discrimination against dollar imports, encouraged "socialist" planning, and subsidized in Europe the monetary support and clearing mechanism that had been rejected for the world when the IMF was set up! Why? Because of the conviction, shared by the majority of the business elite, labor, and the government that systematic efforts to raise living standards and further industrial democracy must be made to head off the appeal of communism.

A favored instrument of multilateral action was the UN Expanded Program of Technical Assistance launched in 1950 with substantial American support. It made no capital funds available; instead, it sent experts to underdeveloped countries to train local specialists and help in setting up development projects. It also financed the training of local specialists abroad. Hand in hand with EPTA went American support for similar pro-

grams run by UN specialized agencies such as WHO, concerned with pub
health; FAO, dealing with agricultural productivity; ILO, training ma.
power; and the UN Children's Fund for famine relief and malnutritior.
None of these instruments involved grants as a long-term method of international development, and the loans remained closely tied to American
interests. Multilateral capital contributions other than technical expert
services were confined to humanitarian gestures and excluded long-range
development aid. Nonetheless, once the door to such noncapitalist participation in world development had been opened, the Third-World countries
quickly sought to pry it ajar even further with a crescendo of demands
for capital aid. These demands had little effect until 1958, but they triggered
a pattern of adjustment by American elites, without which the burgeoning
of UN aid activities in our decade is inconceivable.

Between 1947 and 1958 the United States learned not only to live
with, but to shape, a web of economic interdependence that ran counter
to much of the original intent and commitment. The economically dominant
nation in the world progressively gave up ideological purity in its effort
to gear economic policy to the political objective of fighting communism,
to seek a free world economy for its exports, and to retain a protected
national economy for those segments that claimed inability to compete with
imports. I shall illustrate this lesson in learned inconsistency by discussing
international tariff policy in GATT, monetary policy in the IMF, commodity
regulation, the growing acceptance of economic regionalism, and the evolution of foreign aid policy.

ITO and GATT.   Congress never consented to the ratification of the
Havana Charter, and the ITO never came into existence. The charter had
been a compromise between the rival views summarized above and therefore satisfied few people in the United States. The Senate declined to act,
essentially for the following reasons, as stated by the U.S. Council of the
International Chamber of Commerce:

> It is a dangerous document because it accepts practically all of the policies
> of economic nationalism; because it jeopardizes the free enterprise system
> by giving priority to centralized national governmental planning of foreign
> trade; because it leaves a wide scope to discrimination, accepts the principle
> of economic insulation and in effect commits all members of the ITO to state
> planning for full employment. From the point of view of the U.S., it has the
> further very grave defect of placing this country in a position where it must
> accept discrimination against itself while extending the Most-Favored-Nation
> treatment to all members of the Organization.[2]

Instead, the United States took the lead in an improvised substitute
for the defunct ITO, namely GATT. This agreement provides that import
quotas must be eliminated, that tariffs cannot be raised but must instead
be lowered by means of periodic multilateral negotiating encounters. While
these negotiations are conducted by pairs of countries on an item-by-item
basis, GATT rules stipulate that reductions must be passed on *without
discrimination* by means of the most-favored-nation clause, thus making

---

[2] Quoted in William Diebold, Jr., "The End of the ITO," *Essays in International
~~e.* No. 16, Oct., 1952 (Princeton, N.J.: Princeton University), pp. 20-21.

process multilateral. The United States insisted that concessions must *reciprocal;* i.e., of equal value to both parties. A code of fair trade rules as appended as well. Complaints that tariffs were raised despite agreement or that quotas were reimposed by a member are dealt with by means of a conciliation and arbitration procedure that could make adjustments in trade rules binding on the members. Because the procedures were close to the liberal vision, the Communist countries and many of the underdeveloped nations declined to join. GATT succeeded in appreciably lowering tariff barriers among industrial countries and in adjudicating some major trade disputes.

IMF and World Money. If GATT sidestepped the UN by creating a system favorable to the industrial West, so did the monetary system that was set up under the IMF. Further, this system during the first decade of its life satisfied the needs of nobody. Contrary to American expectations, the IMF did not succeed in persuading all nations to stabilize their par values and to refrain from unilateral revaluation of their currencies. Its dollar reserves proved inadequate to support all balances of payments under pressure. The institutionalized gold-exchange standard intended by the fund soon gave way, *de facto*, to a global dollar-exchange standard that owed its success to policies made outside the IMF. Indeed, the IMF decision-making style stresses the avoidance of sharp basic ideological and theoretical debate. Formal decisions are preceded by private negotiations between staff and national representatives and monetary experts. Although formal votes are not necessary, the United States has never been "defeated"; usually, it had its way during the 1950's.

Commodity Agreements. The United States was able to reject and sidetrack other economic demands not congruent with the remains of the liberal doctrine. The underdeveloped nations and some European countries attempted to use the UN Economic and Social Council, in 1950 and 1951, as a forum for discussing a global approach to employment stability, industrial production, commodity prices, and economic growth—suggesting a modest international economic plan. The United States succeeded in halting these discussions in ECOSOC. The Director-General of the FAO, in alliance with many underdeveloped and food-importing countries, suggested a World Food Board, a buffer stock arrangement under which the FAO would buy up surpluses at minimum prices and sell them at fixed ceilings when shortages occurred, thus stabilizing prices and controlling stocks while having a reserve available for famine relief. The plan was killed by the United States and Britain because of the preference for private trading in agricultural commodities. This attitude has slowed down the conclusion of a series of comprehensive commodity agreements.

Regional Trading Systems. Similarly, the United States opposed the creation of all regional trading and economic development arrangements that seemed to interfere with a global division of labor based on nondiscrimination and reciprocity. In Europe, it opposed the formation of customs unions with purely economic objectives. Elsewhere, it accepted with reluctance the establishment of the UN Economic Commission for Latin America and the more diffuse UN Economic Commission for Asia and the Far East. Both bodies were deprived of decision-making powers and in-

dependent sources of finance; both were simply to discuss regional issu
and engage in technical assistance. It took a sharp change in the inte.
national system to make the United States participate in the creation anc
funding of regional development banks.

But in line with the lesson in inconsistency, one major exception to
economic purity was to gather volume and speed later: the encouragement
of *politically justified* regionalism and discrimination in Europe. The noncapitalist elements implicit in the Marshall Plan were accepted easily because it was thought necessary to depart from free enterprise to combat
communism! American industrialists associated with the Committee for
Economic Development and the National Planning Association made their
peace with this arrangement, on condition that European recovery would
be directed by an experienced industrialist at the head of a separate agency,
rather than by the State Department, which was suspected of administering
a global give-away program. And thus Paul Hoffman became the czar of
European economic cooperation and the legitimator of regional economic
discrimination that was to lead gradually to an American-endorsed West
European federation, while the business fundamentalists who objected to
subsidized socialism abroad went unheeded.

The institutional order in which all this took place was the Organization for European Economic Cooperation (OEEC), in which the United
States was a *very* active observer represented by the autonomous American
aid agency, the Economic Cooperation Administration. OEEC pioneered a
method of intergovernmental discussion and confrontation in which frank
criticism and collective pressure were systematically used to persuade member nations to adjust their economic policies to suit the program of the
collectivity. The United States, at this time the supplier of the system, took
the initiative in enmeshing the Europeans in this web of mutual aid and
consultation. Until the mid-1950's, the world economy was led by the U.S., a
leadership institutionalized in GATT, the OEEC, and the NATO-affiliated
system for the economic boycott of the Soviet bloc, thus effectively cutting
out the UN.

Foreign Aid. All foreign aid can be classified in terms of the aims
the donor has in mind. We can identify aid intended merely to demonstrate
the power and "presence" of the donor in a specific situation. Sometimes
aid is given to influence, once or twice, specific decisions by a foreign
government. Both kinds of aid can take the form of grants, loans, demon-
strations, military equipment, or cultural missions. Whatever the form, the
purpose is confined to the achievement of an immediate and short-run
objective. A third type of aid, called "strategic aid" by Montgomery, is our
major concern. The purpose of the donor here is to contribute to the shaping
of a certain world order, an over-all environment favorable to the values
held dear by the donor.[3] The forms can be all-inclusive; the purpose is
sweeping, long-range, independent of local crises. It is identical with most
multilateral programs entrusted to international organizations.

What, then, were American "strategic" objectives in 1947? The govern-

---

[3] John D. Montgomery, *Foreign Aid in International Politics* (Englewood Cliffs,
N.J.: Prentice-Hall, 1967), pp. 18-23.

ent, the innovative business elite, and labor were one in believing that
1ere was a Soviet military threat to Western Europe, that it was made
worse by the desperation of the European workingman who sought a better
life in the face of war-shattered economies and timid European industrialists
who could not rebuild, modernize, and produce enough, at prices low
enough, to satisfy the population. The purpose of American aid was to
correct these conditions; its underlying ideology was that economic power
could create conditions that would make communism unnecessary—in effect,
an inverse Marxism. In Europe this was relatively simple, since democracy,
industry, modernity, and science already existed and nations had a long and
often bloody identity. But we are not sure whether economic growth in the
Third World must precede democracy or whether the reverse sequence is
preferable. We are unsure whether economic development and democracy
must precede nation-building or whether the nation must exist first. The
omnipotent solvent for nagging doubt about these priorities and uncertain
causal connections is that American foreign aid policy, like foreign trade
policy, is to assure conditions of peace, freedom, stability, and prosperity.
Whether peace depends on prosperity or prosperity on peace, however,
remains beclouded.

Nor was the leap into foreign aid in 1947 based solely on these notions. Specific interests in American society received satisfaction then as
they do now. Farmers were assured that the Marshall Plan would facilitate
the sale of agricultural surpluses in Europe; innovative manufacturers were
told that the economic revival of Europe would provide a better climate
for foreign investments and permit the credo of production-oriented in-
dustrialism to take root; labor leaders were given the opportunity to spread
the gospel of American-style trade unionism, and conservative businessmen
were assured that all this would conduce to strengthening private property,
free enterprise, and conservative fiscal policies in Europe. In short, the
$11 billion aid venture was based on a mixture of very general objectives
and very specific material and moral payoffs to certain elite groups.

Nor should we ever forget that Congress remains a crucial actor in
the foreign aid field, more crucial than in the context of tariff and trade
policy, because the President *must* have congressional approval to finance
his programs. Many congressmen are unwilling to spend heavily for the
benefit of other countries, because they doubt the value of such programs
in achieving American objectives; and in periods of rising taxes, conflicting
domestic programs, and international monetary instability, many simply
prefer to spend American resources for programs closer to home. Moreover,
when crucial domestic groups clash and disagree on proper priorities at
home and abroad and when specific payoffs to key domestic groups become
of questionable value, congressional acquiescence in strong foreign aid programs wanes rapidly.

As if sensing the inconsistency of doctrine and policy, as though the
world's giant should have a guilty conscience about tailoring economic
policy to international political forces and domestic protectionists, some
elite groups began to urge revaluation of the UN as an appropriate global
forum for making economic arrangements of importance to all, and they
asked for a more positive attitude toward regionalism among underdevel-

oped and neutralist countries. Their suggestions, however, were product
only when economic policy was examined in the context of foreign aid ar
development under the pressure of the rising Third World.

THE PASSING OF AMERICAN ECONOMIC DOMINANCE

Since 1958 the enmeshment of the United States in the world economy
has become more real, almost in proportion to a *lack of deliberate will* to
be enmeshed. Certainly a lesson has been learned by the elites who take
a consistent interest in world trade and finance. But it was not a lesson that
grew logically out of the postwar commitment to pure international liberalism. Rather, the lesson learned was that a change in economic and political
conditions may beget an unintended involvement in the policies and good
will of others, an unwilled dependence on their views, an unplanned sub-
servience to institutions and pressures built for different initial purposes.
What are the changes in conditions that triggered all this?

Undoubtedly the most powerful stimulus to American learning was
the revolution of rising expectations in the Third World and its concomitant
demands for more capital aid and a trade policy geared to economic development, not to the export desires of the industrial world. In the face of
this clamor, the majority of Americans in 1954 still wanted all aid handled
bilaterally. Many more wanted aid cut off from countries refusing to cooperate with the United States. In 1954, the prestigious Randall Commission
reported to Congress that "underdeveloped areas are claiming a right to
economic aid from the United States. . . . We recognize no such right." [4]
In 1957, 61 per cent of the American people wished to reduce the American
contribution to all kinds of programs.

Thus between 1948 and 1955, the United States fought off bitter complaints from the Third World that technical assistance and IBRD loans
were quite insufficient to enable the developing nations to "catch up," to
bring about some measure of global income redistribution. Third-World
arguments in UN bodies, like arguments of the United States, insisted on
some vague link between "peace" and "prosperity"—though they omitted
any public suggestion of the supposedly stabilizing influence of anticommunist development programs. Indeed, the Third World's emotional clamor
for aid in industrialization was based on no more elaborate objectives and
consistent purposes than the American approach. Yet the United States,
asserting its free trade and enterprise vision, still prevailed against the
clamor.

What were the components of this clamor? One was the demand for
a large-scale UN development program based on outright grants to developing nations, designed to underwrite national industrialization plans,
rather than loans tied to specific improvement projects (such as rail lines,
dams, or foreign exchange-earning industries) as disbursed by the IBRD.
The other was the insistence on special investment policies and trading rules
for regions of underdeveloped nations, notably in Latin America, in order

---

[4] Quoted in L. K. Hyde, *The United States and the United Nations: Promoting the
Public Welfare* (New York: Manhattan Publishing Co., 1966), p. 144.

have aid take the form of protecting countries in the early stages of industrialization from the self-serving aid measures and aggressive sales practices of the industrial countries. The regionalist argument was the special province of the UN Economic Commission for Latin America in its search to protect the struggling countries at the "periphery" of world trade from the rapacious giants at the "center." It failed to arouse American interest in special regional development programs until Castro's Cuba triggered the reaction we now call the Alliance for Progress.

In every session of all appropriate UN organs from 1951 on, capital aid on easy terms was demanded as a function of "SUNFED." As these resolutions were offered, the United States opposed them with a variety of arguments. They would feed irresponsible projects and hurt sound financial practices; they would aid socialist planning at the expense of private capital; the necessary funds were not available; world disarmament would have to precede the mobilization of adequate funds. Whatever the argument, the United States did not retreat from its position, shared as it was by most of the other industrial nations of the West; and yet the Third World did not give up its onslaught. As the Soviet Union turned more and more to UN agencies for its international programs and verbal overtures, as the Korean War ended, and as the Third World made its massive entry into the international system during the mid-Fifties, things seemed to be stalemated.

A very different change was the direct result of American foreign aid, loans abroad, and the stationing of large numbers of American troops in Europe and Asia: the balance-of-payments crisis that has plagued American foreign economic relations since 1958. As the outflow of dollars—private and governmental—continued, the claims of a burgeoning world trading community for dollars as the major means of settling accounts began to put a strain on the monetary resources of even the world's giant. Gold left the United States in large amounts in settlement of accounts, and not sufficient new gold was mined or imported to fill the gap. "Euro-dollars" was the term Europe bestowed on dollars used as a standard means of moving capital while the pound sterling continued its decline from its former position as a major world currency. Given this condition, Washington lost the special power it had previously enjoyed as the major supplier of hard currency that aided in relieving the balance of payments crises of others; the United States now needed the help of its former clients.

Moreover, those former clients soon became the single largest bloc of world traders. The six European continental industrial nations united in the European Economic Community (EEC), recovered from war, re-equipped, freed from colonial responsibilities, were now determined to export their sophisticated manufactures and protect their high-cost agriculture by discriminating against American exports. They were joined by Japan as a new and major industrial competitor of the United States. Europe's new economic independence and prowess also triggered a certain fear of American direct investments as interference with European planning; yet Europeans also feared being deprived of superior American technological and scientific skills if they excluded American capital, and they feared being victimized further by the brain drain of their technicians to America. In

short, Europe's prowess also implied ambivalence and soul-searching abo**
the proper relations among the Atlantic nations—attitudes that had the
counterparts in a drifting policy in NATO.

The revolt of the Third World, aided verbally by the Soviet bloc,
dramatically shook the hegemonic position of the United States in the world
economy. The Third World used the UN as the chief forum for denouncing
the economic policies of the West. As it gained victory after victory in the
General Assembly and the specialized agencies, American elite opinion began to question the continued utility of the UN as a vehicle of American
policy; it seemed to become the forum for demonstrating American economic isolation instead.

Yet the malaise of the business community with respect to the anti-
capitalist demands of the Third World in the UN stopped short of down-
grading the UN completely. Certain innovating industrialists had suggested
as early as 1951 that the IBRD approach economic development in less
conservative terms and deal directly with private firms abroad. Local
opinion leaders, especially businessmen, were increasingly accepting foreign
aid by the mid-Fifties, even arguing for more of it in many cases. American
learning was undoubtedly heavily influenced by the views of this "passionate minority," and the UN profited therefrom. European elites by contrast
experienced no such tolerance and frankly preferred to sidestep UN procedures and institutions. The centerpiece of the Third World's revolt was
the claim that the GATT–IMF world economic rules hide a fundamental
discrimination *de facto* against the export earnings of developing nations
by allowing all sorts of indirect and covert financial burdens on the sale
of their primary and manufactured goods, refusing to make capital available
on any but sound banking principles, and by declining to stabilize the
prices of primary commodities.

What, then, have Americans learned from this onslaught? They have
learned to upgrade, slowly and incrementally, the type and amount of
foreign aid administered by the UN and to allow the UN a larger role in
planning aid programs. They have reluctantly acquiesced in a reform of
world trading rules that come closer to linking economic development and
international trade into a coherent whole, and they have accepted a new
international institution—UNCTAD—as the chief actor. And finally, they
have reconsidered the principle of regionalism, both as a focus for economic
development and as a principle of political organization for shaping it.

THE THIRD-WORLD CHALLENGE AND THE
INSTITUTIONAL RESPONSE: FOREIGN AID

America's response was eventually to take the form of expanding foreign aid until the plateau of the mid-Sixties was reached *without* opting
finally in favor of bilateral or multilateral assistance, but supporting both.
If aid designed to impress, bribe, or cajole a foreign regime remained entirely bilateral, not all of the strategic foreign aid was given to UN agencies
either. Hence, although reasons militating in favor of multilateral strategic
aid were adduced more commonly after 1956, the major response of the

▄ted States to the lessons of the early Fifties was merely to accede to
▄ creation of new UN institutions in the foreign aid field, without endow-
▄g them with all the financial potency desired by the developing nations
▄nd without detracting from continued bilateral activity. Further, from 1962
on, the conditions attached to bilateral aid became increasingly tied to the
needs of the American economy.

Since the IBRD was the favored instrument of multilateral aid, it is
not surprising that the United States sought to meet the Third World
challenge simply by enlarging and legitimating a broader development task
for the bank. The first sign that the Republican Administration might be
willing to depart from its premises came in 1955. U.S. Treasury officials and
leading bankers and businessmen professed to feel increasingly uneasy over
the image they were creating abroad by unbroken American resistance to
the SUNFED idea; this uneasiness was increased by persistent reports by
American delegates to UN sessions observing the bad image. Once this
aura existed, Eugene Black took the initiative in persuading Administration
leaders that a flexible IBRD policy of investing in private enterprise abroad,
without insisting on government guarantees of soundness, would aid development, free enterprise, and America's international reputation. Thus was
born the idea for an affiliate for the bank, the International Finance Corpo-
ration (IFC).

But the creation of IFC did not stop the demand for SUNFED. And
again it was the bank that used its prestige in American elite circles to
espouse the idea of enlarging its loan activity by acquiring a new affiliate
able to make soft loans: the International Development Association (IDA).
Multipurpose, low-interest loans repayable in local currencies would be
made to nations already so burdened with repayment and interest charges
that they no longer constituted bankable risks for the IBRD. Although
Black supported the idea, public initiative came from Senator Mike Monroney (D., Okla.). SUNFED agitation in the UN, via the quiet pressure of
the IBRD in Washington, had influenced the senator to push for a new
American approach to foreign aid. Monroney stressed that IDA would remove economic development from domestic American political debate and
save the United States money by mobilizing soft foreign currencies more
effectively. Internationally, Monroney stressed that IDA would remove the
political stigma that attaches to nationally administered loans, give the
recipient nations a voice and an opportunity to learn the virtues of long-
range financial planning, in which they could help each other through the
use of local currencies. Black and the IBRD welcomed the scheme because
of the improved image; American aid notables favored it because it seemed
to head off the dreaded SUNFED. IDA proceeded to become a very soft-
hearted bank indeed!

IFC and IDA do not exhaust the adaptability of the IBRD and its
American friends. George Woods, Black's successor as president of the
family of lending institutions, continued the subtle mixture of hard and
soft banking policies but expressed more sympathy than Black felt for soft
lending and support of state enterprises. Woods altered the bank's own
policies by allowing very long-term loans, increasing IDA resources from
the parent's earnings. He also veered toward the country approach to

TABLE 7 · *UNITED STATES FOREIGN AID: BILATERAL VS.*
MULTILATERAL 1956-1965 (dollars are in millions)

	1956	1960	1962	1963	1964	1965
TOTAL FLOW OF PUBLIC FINANCIAL RESOURCES [a]	$2,006	$2,834	$3,671	$3,755	$3,462	$3,730
Total net bilateral flow	$1,440 [b]	$2,540 [c]	–	$3,557 [d]	$3,188 [d]	$3,462 [d]
Total net multilateral flow	$ 566 [b]	$ 294 [c]	–	$ 198 [d]	$ 274 [d]	$ 267 [d]
Multilateral flow as per cent of total	28%	10%	–	5%	8%	7%
TOTAL FLOW OF PUBLIC TECHNICAL ASSISTANCE	–	–	$ 454	$ 452	$ 515	$ 490
Total net bilateral technical assistance	–	–	$ 413 [e]	$ 424 [e]	$ 433 [e]	$ 466 [e]
Total net multilateral technical assistance [e]	$ 14 [f]	–	$ 41 [e]	$ 28 [e]	$ 82 [e]	$ 24 [e]
Multilateral flow as per cent of total	–	–	9%	6%	16%	5%

[a] OECD, *Development Assistance Efforts and Policies: 1966 Review*, Table 2, p. 148.
[b] U.S. Fiscal Year 1956-57, UN doc. E/3131, par. 86.
[c] *International Conciliation*, No. 534 (Sept., 1961), p. 140.
[d] OECD, *op. cit.*, Tables 5, 6, 7, pp. 152-57.
[e] OECD, *op. cit.*, Table 11, pp. 162-63.
[f] *International Conciliation*, No. 514 (Sept., 1957), p. 131.
– Not available.

development assistance, away from the more limiting project approach. Further, he encouraged receiving countries to put their loan requests into the context of comprehensive economic planning and even talked about the need for a UN development plan in order to rationalize and improve allocation of the world's lending resources. The bank also began to support agricultural and education projects. IBRD even assumed delicate political tasks, such as the organization of international financial consortia to develop the Indus Valley, produce Iranian oil, and refinance the Suez Canal, contrary to American intentions in 1944 but eventually with Washington's blessings.

But the IBRD was still a long way from being a capital aid fund under the control of the Third World. Nor did these reforms and adaptations still the demand for SUNFED. Washington had attempted to use the specialized agencies to approximate Third-World demands without actually creating an independent capital aid fund. Thus, in addition to the extensive technical assistance operations carried out by the specialized agencies, the United States enthusiastically supported operational programs such as WHO's malaria eradication campaigns, UNESCO's basic education pro-

ıms in Latin America and Africa, ILO's manpower training programs,
ıd—most important—the FAO-run World Food Program. As initiated in
962 and extended in 1965, this program seeks to use food surpluses for
development. Nations with surplus food donate it; others may donate cash
or shipping services. These resources are then allotted to developing nations
able to use food as a component in specific development projects or to stave
off famine. During the first three years, $100 million were spent; for the
second three-year period, $275 million are targeted. Why did the United
States agree to this, despite its opposition to UN-run commodity programs?
It endorsed the World Food Program as an alternative preferable to a rival
scheme advocated by Canada, the Third World, and FAO: a comprehensive
commodity plan that would have included price and marketing arrangements as well as aid to developing nations and that would have taken the
place of the bilateral American Food-for-Peace Program. Because the rival
plan was to reach proportions of $12 billion, it would have effectively re-
moved from the world market vast quantities of food and thereby contributed to price stability while making free food available to the poorest
nations.

Since none of these cautious concessions succeeded in reducing the
clamor for SUNFED or in giving the United States a more benign image,
more incremental adaptation was felt to be necessary, though no massive
conversion to the SUNFED idea or the principle of radical income redistribution occurred. A major step was the idea launched by Paul Hoffman
in 1958 to combine the rationalization of specialized agency technical
assistance with increased investment in nonbankable enterprises. The term
pre-investment was chosen in order not to offend opponents of the soft
approach. Emphasis was to be placed on surveys of resources and educational facilities in relation to industrialization plans, the examination of
such plans, and the intercession of the UN in obtaining public or private
funding for them. This program took shape in the form of the United
Nations Special Fund. Its operations considerably increased technical assistance pre-investment resources and extended control over the entire UN
technical assistance program by making the specialized agencies dependent
on central funding. In so doing, it met the American insistence on stream-
lining specialized agency operations and avoiding overlaps. In American
eyes, the Special Fund was so successful that Washington advanced the
idea of having it assume officially all UN development assistance other than
IBRD–IFC–IDA operations and having it direct the specialized agencies'
assistance programs under the label UN Development Program. In 1965
UNDP, under Hoffman, was set up, even though the Third World regretted
the centralization. Nor did it stop its demand for SUNFED.

A few years earlier, the Third World had demanded the creation of
a new, specialized agency to be devoted to making grants for the stimulation of industry, another version of SUNFED. The United States was opposed to this venture, too, but eventually supported a watered-down version
of it when the UNCTAD came out strongly for an industrial development
agency. A small Center for Industrial Development, with an ambiguous
mandate and a very small budget, was created in the UN Secretariat. Industrialization, Washington felt, was too important an issue to be left to the

domination of others. In 1965 the General Assembly unanimously voted t create another autonomous agency under its control, the UN Industria Development Organization (UNIDO), a compromise between the full-fledged specialized agency demanded by the developing nations and the small Center preferred by the West. It is ruled by a 45-nation Industrial Development Board, the majority of which represents underdeveloped members. UNIDO has a very broad task. It aids all phases of industrialization, pre-investment, training and education, and the marketing of processed, primary, and manufactured goods; it contributes to national and regional planning and seeks to help in changing rules governing industrial property in order to accelerate the diffusion of technological knowledge. Even though in 1967 it was decided to finance UNIDO from UNDP funds at first, its program thus may well compete directly with the UNDP's and the specialized agencies, especially if pressure to make it into a plain capital aid fund were to succeed.

THE THIRD-WORLD CHALLENGE AND THE
INSTITUTIONAL RESPONSE: MONEY AND TRADE

It is far from easy to define the objectives of American foreign trade policy since 1955 except as an inchoate collection of slogans, partly derived from economic liberalism and partly inferred from the politics of the Cold War. This "basic sextet of goals" is summed up by Michael Brower: "peace, security, freedom (or liberty), justice, well-being and prosperity." [5] The major aim of policy after the mid-Fifties became the acceleration of economic growth in developing nations, because poverty was viewed as a threat to the sextet of goals. Such acceleration was expected somehow to further the attainment of democratic institutions abroad and assure sufficient economic stability to permit security, peace, and freedom to prevail. This collection of slogans lacks internal consistency and rests on very superficial thinking. Yet there can be little doubt that government and private elites accepted it as a fair statement of the new American vision after American hegemony began to wane. Nor can there be any doubt of the business elite's predominant commitment to lower tariffs and stepped-up trade.

Thus, the doubling of the IMF's reserves in 1959 was not opposed by a single interest group, and it was supported by all the chief associations of labor, bankers, farmers, and business, even though ten years earlier such unanimity would hardly have existed. President Kennedy sought to equate peace, prosperity, and freedom with the military strength of the Atlantic countries in proposing a 50 per cent cut in tariffs between the United States and the EEC (by virtue of the Trade Expansion Act of 1962 and the subsequent Kennedy Round at GATT). His initiative was supported by every major economic interest group and many humanitarian and public service associations; opposition came chiefly from associations of specialized manufacturers that would lose their tariff protection (piano makers, the watch

[5] Quoted and developed in Benjamin Higgins, *The United Nations and U.S. Foreign Economic Policy* (Homewood, Ill.: Irwin, 1962), pp. 3-4.

industry, bicycle manufacturers) and from the labor unions affiliated with these industries. The AFL-CIO, however, equated the world and the national interest with increased foreign aid and with expanded trade (provided trade adjustment assistance was given to those hurt by lowered tariffs). Labor also wanted the UN to negotiate a code for the protection of private foreign investments abroad. Farmers were quite content with the Kennedy approach as long as some surplus food stocks were removed from the world market by means of grants of food to needy nations (financed by the government under Public Law 480 and the World Food Program), and provided that foreign food be kept out of the United States while export markets in Western Europe remained open. No party and no major group challenged the notion that increased trade, lower tariffs, a stronger world monetary system would all conduce to peace, American and world prosperity, Atlantic unity, free enterprise, weakened Communist appeals in the Third World, democracy, and stability. If the approach was less orthodox and less doctrinaire than in 1945, it was also less consistent and more indebted to liberal wishful thinking. It did rest, however, on a clear—if sloppy—consensus of the American elites.

If there was something of a plan in 1945, by the end of the Fifties its traces had been well obscured. Learning took the form of step-by-step, issue-by-issue adjustment. No new central institution was set up, though new tasks were added to the disparate collection of separate forums. No sweeping and rational review of trade and monetary policy took place. Incremental accommodations to a changing international environment occurred with respect to monetary policy, revision of the GATT rules, acceptance of the legitimacy of regional trade blocs and regulations, and the trade demands of the Third World, which called for and received its own forum for action in the UN Conference on Trade and Development (UNCTAD). Whether these accommodations have resulted in further enmeshments must now be determined.

The development of a dollar-exchange standard had condemned the IMF to a peripheral role in monetary affairs until, in 1958, the United States reversed policy and began a campaign of solving its payments problems with a reinvigorated world monetary system in the IMF. In effect, the United States wished to resign the role of being the world's central banker and bequeath it to the very IMF that had been denied the role because of American fears in 1944. This decision was made as a result of several developments. As the outflow of gold and dollars continued, the major European currencies, strong once more, all became convertible. As world trade was growing by leaps and bounds, it was in fact being financed with the American dollar and gold outflow, despite the comeback of EEC currencies, thus linking American problems with a worldwide shortage of money; this is the so-called liquidity problem. Further, the EEC countries now told the United States to combat its gold and dollar losses with a policy of domestic deflation and retrenchment, a policy not acceptable to the United States because of the increased unemployment that would result.

How to rescue the dollar and provide liquidity? No permanent solution has been found, though the United States in 1965 proposed a radical plan for a greatly strengthened IMF that would provide automatic checking account privileges to the world's trading nations. The accounts would operate with a new international currency backed by all strong currencies, in addition to gold and dollars, to be called Special Drawing Rights or SDR's.

General agreement on this major reform was achieved in 1968 when all the major trading nations of the world accepted the issuing of SDR's by the IMF in allotments proportional to the present national subscriptions of funds. The IMF is to distribute the new international currency equitably to developed and developing nations. The fund determines the basic timing, amount, and rate of allocation of SDR's. Important decisions will require a majority of 85 per cent, a figure that can be met by the combined vote of the European Economic Community nations and the United States; less important decisions will be made by simple majority. The staff of the IMF, however, will have important new powers of initiating steps and advising the Board of Governors. Clearly, the scheme moves the world considerably in the direction of a global central banking system and thereby makes American monetary policy much more dependent than ever before on the policies of other nations and international organizations. The trauma suffered by the flood of gold leaving the United States in 1967 and 1968 drove home this dependence and made the remedy more acceptable. But the United States had to pay a price: just when we were prepared to seek our salvation through enmeshment, the major trading partners in OECD's Group of Ten (seven European nations, Canada, Japan, and the United States) were inclined to support the new American policy only if taxes were raised, consumption curbed, and the payments deficit controlled. Because the Group of Ten had agreed to a series of measures that involved supporting the dollar and strengthening the IMF, the success of the new system would depend on continued harmony of views and policies in the Group. The renewed crisis of the French economy and continued weakness of the British pound and French franc contrasted to the German mark illustrate that this harmony cannot be taken for granted.

American desire to reform world institutions is much less in evidence when we turn to trade policy and to the accommodation of the Third World's demands. The developing nations, backed by the Soviet bloc, mounted nothing less than a revolt against the dominant GATT rules at UNCTAD I in 1964, an encounter described by a high American official as "the first major international conference in recent history in which the East-West confrontation was submerged by the North-South confrontation." Over the bitter dissent of the United States, the cohesive and well-organized bloc of 77 developing nations succeeded in bringing about the adoption of these major resolutions: commodity agreements should be drafted to stabilize prices; the developed countries should give discriminatory, preferential tariff concessions to the Third-World countries by allowing the importation of their manufactures; the principle of reciprocity should be abandoned in tariff bargaining, to allow the developing nations greater export earnings; the right of Third-World nations to dispose of their natural resources is absolute, thus exposing foreign investors to the threat of nationalization. While these resolutions have not become part of the world trading rules, the effort to enforce them has now been given to a permanent 45-nation

UN Trade Development Board which, unlike GATT, is not under the control of the developed nations. The new forum is a watershed in American trade policy in international organizations, even though at UNCTAD II in 1968 the United States conceded far less than demanded of it. The extent of the American adjustment can be illustrated by the policies urged and adopted in GATT, that "soulless forum of the rich" in the rhetoric of the Third World.

A Presidential Report in 1957 reiterated the importance of GATT to U.S. foreign policy:

> Experience through the years has demonstrated clearly the superiority of multilateral discussions and negotiations over bilateral in achieving the objectives of U.S. policy in these fields.[6]

Multilateral commercial diplomacy for the U.S. meant strictly reciprocal trade concessions negotiated for selective items, administered nondiscriminatorily among nations. The U.S. rejected across-the-board tariff negotiations at GATT, partly because the President was empowered by Congress to reduce tariffs only up to a limit of 15 per cent over a three-year period. Congress was also hostile to the idea of linear tariff cuts, because they would reduce its influence over tariff schedules on particular items. "The U.S. was a prisoner of its domestic legislation." [7] The emergence of the EEC as a major economic force plus America's increasing balance of payments deficit forced U.S. policy-makers to change their position on linear tariff reductions. Across-the-board reductions were at the heart of the 1962 Trade Expansion Act. Linear reduction as a method of commercial policy is not a blessing to states interested in limited tariff cuts. It is positively discriminatory against developing nations, still dependent on exports of primary commodities but anxious to find a new market for their still high-priced infant manufactures. Hence the American conversion to the linear reduction method in GATT in relation to other industrial nations did nothing to reassure the Third World.

The success of the Kennedy Round at GATT, then, merely confirms the part of the American approach that stresses nondiscriminatory trade liberalization and reciprocal benefits. Johnson Administration negotiators held that one major utility of GATT for the United States lay in its availability as a forum for nondiscriminatory tariff reduction, "nondiscriminatory" for the Third World too. Some American officials make clear that GATT keeps the preferential trading systems of Europe and Latin America under control by surveying their policies and giving third countries the opportunity to protest and retaliate if regional preferences pass the bounds of permissibility. When, in anticipation of UNCTAD, the GATT membership adopted an Action Program in 1963 that seemed to give some satisfaction to the complaints of the Third World, the United States made few and halting adjustments in its trade policy in line with the recommendations. It then refused to sanction the principle of preferential duties for developing nations' manufactures and made minimal tariff reductions to accommodate

---

[6] *Department of State Bulletin* (Nov. 4, 1957), p. 725.

[7] Gerald Curzon, *Multilateral Commercial Diplomacy* (London: Michael Joseph, 1966), p. 95.

more imports of primary products. It continued, along with the EEC, to practice outright quota protectionism for agricultural imports. And it declined to generalize to other products the agreement on cotton textiles, concluded in GATT with the countries of East Asia. During the Kennedy Round itself, American negotiators insisted that these talks assured benefits for developing nations merely by virtue of their insistence on most-favored-nation treatment. As it turned out, the Kennedy Round resulted in a 37 per cent average reduction of tariffs of industrial countries, reducing them to a level of 9 per cent! By the time UNCTAD II met in 1968, the chink in the armor of pure free trade was growing visibly as the United States further changed its policy on preferences to developing nations: Washington conceded that it now favored tariff preferences for goods manufactured by developing nations, provided the preferences were "generalized," i.e., offered by *all* industrial nations to *all* developing nations without discrimination, thus maintaining some export competition and preventing the creation of new uneconomic preferences. Washington also agreed that GATT relax the insistence on reciprocity in tariff negotiations. By 1968, the United States told UNCTAD II that commodity agreements for sugar, cocoa, and wheat were also appropriate and that the principle of commodity regulation should be followed more energetically, insuring against loss of export earning in the event of growth of synthetics. Therefore, commodity agreements should be tied to schemes for giving exporting countries incentives for the diversification of monocultural practices. The icy façade of free trade doctrine seemed to be melting as UNCTAD II was told that development "requires an international harmonization of economic policies, the discipline of development plans, changes in structure and attitude both in the developed and developing countries. . . ." [8]

THE THIRD-WORLD CHALLENGE AND
THE ACCEPTANCE OF REGIONALISM

Perhaps the most telling lesson learned by the United States was the inevitability of regionalism in a world in which trade, aid, and politics simply would not remain in tight and separate compartments. Free trade areas and common markets in Latin America were accepted by Washington, it must be stressed, as proper and legitimate—though discriminatory and preferential—methods of industrialization. The endorsement of, and financial participation in, development banks in Asia, Africa, and Latin America was a milestone in American adjustment to a world bent on limiting free trade and private capital movements. But all these steps involved no serious enmeshment of the United States, since the institutions concerned were under the control of others and only marginally related to American interests—and GATT remained to criticize them. In the Atlantic region, however, the story is different. Here enmeshment may play a much larger role.

"Like Pirandello's six characters in search of an author, the policy-makers sometimes appear to be casting about for more topical settings of

[8] Eugene V. Rostow, "From Aid to Cooperation," *Department of State Bulletin* (March 11, 1968), p. 360.

such stereotyped subjects as 'trade blocs,' 'Atlantic community,' even—alas—the western alliance itself." [9] The slogans have been with us since the Marshall Plan; the new topical setting is the OECD. Is it more than a slogan with a headquarters? All-European integration of the most federalist type was the preferred American objective, and until the Sixties everything was subordinated to it. Few people in Washington stopped to inquire whether an *independently* strong and united Europe was a desirable development. Until de Gaulle made the point for America, little thought had been given to which of two rival European trade blocs should be supported. As late as 1962, President Kennedy believed that the partnership formula would paper things over nicely when joined to dramatic increases in Atlantic trade.

What was the United States after, in founding OECD? It was *not* interested in general trade policy and wanted no part of the OEEC Code of Liberalization. Congress in 1960 was so hostile to any fixed trade rules that it made the Administration demand the scrapping of the Code. Congress was accustomed to GATT and therefore tolerated its item-by-item approach; in 1961 it did not want to give the Administration increased blanket powers over trade of the kind that Kennedy did get in 1962. The OECD voting formula, further, assured that the U.S. would not assume blanket trade obligations. Because of the balance of payments troubles and the desire to cut back the dollar outflow to Europe, the United States was interested in burden-sharing for foreign aid as well as in the discussion of growth rates and harmonized growth. Officially, at least, Washington was not interested in the little-known technique of intergovernmental scrutiny, discussion, confrontation, and harmonization invented by OEEC. Consequently, the powers given to the OECD were vague and general compared to those of the predecessor, OEEC. The Senate Foreign Relations Committee, in its report favoring ratification of the OECD Charter, stressed only the sharing of aid and the joint Atlantic promotion of economic growth. Nondiscriminatory world trade development as an American objective was played down in order to leave this task with GATT. A high official defined the job intended for OECD:

> Cooperation in the OECD is not usually aimed at the development of uniform national policies. The consultative process leaves ample room for differences in policies stemming from varying emphasis of national objectives and multiplicity of national circumstances. The primary aim of policy coordination in the OECD is to ensure that national policies develop in step with each other.[10]

The advent of UNCTAD and the transformation of GATT have nevertheless enmeshed the United States in general trade discussions in OECD, as an unanticipated consequence of the Third World's revolt and the growing interest of some European nations in granting preferential tariff treatment. Although no startling Atlantic trade policy has emerged from the intensive discussion in OECD, there is some evidence that the organization is being converted into an "antechamber" in which the industrial nations

[9] Henry G. Aubrey, *Atlantic Economic Cooperation* (New York: Praeger, 1967), pp. 3-4.

[10] William R. Tyler, Assistant Secretary of State for European Affairs, quoted in *ibid.*, pp. 103-4.

concert their approach for the global encounters elsewhere in the web of international organizations. What is more striking is the entirely unintended enmeshment of the United States in OECD discussions of economic growth and domestic economic policies needed for growth. The OEEC confrontation technique was carried over bodily into OECD—and the United States was made one of the victims as the payments deficit created a stronger need to harmonize economic policies with the European consumers of dollars. It was in OECD discussions that the Group of Ten negotiated its reserve currency standby agreement and OECD studies and talks were used to launch tax cuts and investment controls in the United States, as well as take up the matter of policies to guarantee minimum incomes. Europe came to understand—even if it could not change—certain inconsistencies in American policy, and American policy-makers whose ideas for change were blocked in Washington found collective allies and supporters for the alterations they wished to introduce at home. "In fact, as practitioners of multilateral diplomacy in the OECD and elsewhere have found on many occasions, an acquired habit of viewing problems from angles other than one's own does promote a search for acceptable solutions, and at the same time makes conflicting interests seem less divergent than they appeared initially." [11]

The United States felt it necessary to use and submit to the confrontation procedure, to explain its own aid policies, and to persuade the Europeans and Japanese to contribute more as they grew richer. This step brought important results, as embarrassment compelled Canada and Britain, among others, to step up their aid. The United States used OECD to organize European aid consortia to shore up the economies of Greece and Turkey and, incidentally, to prescribe strict rules for the economic conduct of the two recipients. OECD thus became known as the Rich Men's Club in the aid as well as in the trade field. Through its Development Assistance Committee, it "deals always with the line at which the edge of one donor's program is in contact with that of another, with problems that are common to nations which have increasingly made aid a part of their national long-range policy." [12] But it does not give multilateral aid itself or prescribe common rules for the bilateral assistance provided by its members. Nor does it coordinate important matters of differences in national approach; instead, it concentrates on minor items on which the donors can agree. The level of interest rates, amortization terms, and grace periods on loans provide such cases of successful coordination. If it is a Rich Men's Club, it is not an effective one, because it has not been successful in influencing the basic political objectives and techniques underlying national donor efforts.

ENMESHMENT, LEARNING, AND THE FUTURE

And so the world's economic giant has found it useful to engage itself in more and softer aid machinery, in regional consultations and aid efforts, in a stronger world monetary system, and in a forum to renegotiate the

[11] Aubrey, *Atlantic Economic Cooperation*, p. 148.
[12] Seymour J. Rubin, *The Conscience of the Rich Nations* (New York: Harper, 1966), pp. 19-20.

basic rules of world trade. As the clamor of the Third World is listened to more attentively in Washington, GATT will have little left to do, especially since the Kennedy Round eliminated the bulk of tariffs in trade among industrial nations.

Still, no new set of trade and money rules has emerged. As the Third World continues its demands for dramatic global redistribution of income and resources, a shift in institutional enmeshment can be gleaned from the welter of activity, but no consensus on aid policy can be seen. Europe is prepared to meet the demand in ways very different from America's. Trade and aid still go their separate ways, undoing each other's tasks on occasion. The United States may yet find it necessary and desirable to grant developing nations extensive compensatory financial assistance for commodity price instability in the IMF and in other types of commodity agreements, in order to make trade take the place of some aid. The curtain has just begun to lift on the retreat from free trade and private investment; before the retreat becomes a chaotic rout, the United States may come to prefer more overlapping between domestic and international economic issues and may quietly bequeath the resulting task of reconciliation to an international organization.

But this possibility is itself the result of planlessness and uncertainty of purpose. The United States is not certain *why* aid is desirable and *how* trade practices and aid objectives can be linked. Nor does it know *when* and *where* multilateral channels should be preferred over bilateral ones in the giving of strategic aid. "The choice for the United States between giving aid bilaterally and giving aid through international organs is a pragmatic one," says Richard N. Gardner, a former State Department official. "The test is which route is more likely to achieve the purposes for which the particular kind of assistance is being granted." [13] This begs the question. Gardner enumerates reasons why multilateral aid is increasingly gaining favor, but he does not clarify the purpose of the aid: recognition of independence and neutrality of new nations, the wider choice of expert personnel and contributing funds, and the tendency to strengthen the autonomy of international organizations as "instruments of peace and welfare." [14]

Pragmatism indeed: American officials favor a doctrine that explains strategic economic aid as furthering "political development" in recipient nations; but they cannot agree on whether "political development" means anticommunism, pro-Americanism, or attachment to peaceful change. Further, they cannot explain *how* economic aid is able to realize these political objectives as long as it is evaluated largely in economic terms; in practice, the objectives of a country's program come to mean "economic growth in the short run." The expectations of the professional aid bureaucrat and his political superiors are much more modest than those of Congress and the major elites. Hence they prefer not to deal directly with the political objectives underlying foreign aid because they distrust their own ability to influence politics abroad decisively with foreign aid measures.[15] Sometimes

[13] Richard N. Gardner, *In Pursuit of World Order, op. cit.,* p. 116.
[14] *Ibid.,* p. 117.
[15] Robert A. Packenham, "Political Development Doctrines in the American Foreign Aid Program," *World Politics* (Jan., 1966), pp. 194-235.

a pragmatic consensus seems to be much the same as a lack of consensus among the very people most in need of clarity of purpose.

Policy-makers and specialists have learned and adjusted; that is, they have bent with the international storm without acquiring a clear new direction. But the business community shows little evidence of accepting institutional enmeshment, continued global income redistribution, or world economic planning; some regard even the various versions of SUNFED now enacted as a kind of development blackmail.

Nor is Congress decisively in favor of these new objectives and methods that deliberately use foreign aid and trade as tools of social engineering. IDA was supported as a "sound" multilateral institution, preferable to bilateral methods, but "sound" because it avoided the more global planning stance. Yet when Congress was asked to extend the life of IDA and re-plenish its coffers, the necessary legislation was passed in 1964 only after initial defeat and in a package deal including important domestic legislation. Since that time, acceptance of foreign aid and enthusiasm for freer trade have both suffered severe setbacks in Congress. There is as little enthusiasm on Capitol Hill as elsewhere for the trend toward autonomous UN capital aid agencies, organs that are seen as politicizing economic development activity and detracting from the sober work of the specialized agencies. Congress tends to feel that American-initiated politicization, such as opposition to the admission of Communist China, is quite permissible, whereas similar efforts by other nations are not. Development has been perceived by Congress as part of the fight against communism. The continuation of multilateral aid under declining American control, in the face of the East-West *détente,* makes little sense to many legislators. A new and broader justification for such aid has yet to be widely accepted.

And why should such a sentiment arise? Americans have been assured that trade and aid will stabilize volatile nations, establish democracy, help free private enterprise abroad, teach economic planning, defeat communism, help in nation-building, and aid the American farmer, educator, and industrialist. They see, however, that these objectives appear to conflict and are diluted in practice by Congress and the Executive. They see further that very little of this seems actually to be realized in aid operations. They do not always understand that short-run and long-run aims may well conflict, that democracy in a generation's time can be built—perhaps—on the basis of an aid-supported military dictatorship today. But since the objectives of the UN are hardly more explicit or consistent, the rational choices of means and instruments are not made easier by the mere fact that the balance of persuasive power has shifted in favor of the UN. We must conclude therefore that the very ambiguity surrounding the objectives and successes of foreign economic policy make it more difficult for a new cohesive American consensus to arise.

In reality, the challenge for American policy must be the recognition that with improvement of *some* living standards, silent frustrations will break out into open rebellion, thus making the revolution of rising expectations the archenemy of economic aid. And one may thus have to conclude that our growing enmeshment in these institutions will lead to the attainment of none of the many objectives of strategic foreign aid unless a far more cohesive policy toward *planned* aid and trade is adopted.

Such a plan must be calculated to achieve the basic American objectives of a prosperous world in which the individual can improve his lot with a minimum of coercion, violence, and manipulation by impersonal political and technological forces. More aid could easily be given by the United States if the OECD-endorsed target of annual contributions equal to 1 per cent of gross national product is to be met. American aid has not reached that target in recent years. If the principle of the progressive income tax were used to compute national contributions to IDA, the United States could be responsible for 65 per cent of the funds instead of the 43 per cent actually contributed. UNIDO and the Capital Development Fund could be generously supported without making them into giant give-aways if the distribution and evaluation of aid were made the collective responsibility of the recipients and donors, as it was in the OEEC under the Marshall Plan. Furthermore, an increase in the multilateral aid component would reduce the uneconomic practice of tying aid funds, which continues to flourish. Economic aid intended to contribute to stability, prosperity, and peace in long-range terms is the shared objective of the United States and the UN. Why not increase the UN share of such aid, since there is no conflict of objectives? Moreover, UN-administered aid has distinct advantages over bilateral measures: it will restore the notion of a master plan for world betterment that was lost early in UN history, and the United States will be prominently associated with this revival; countries resisting the strings of bilateral Soviet or American aid would have a multilateral program large enough to suit them if America's professions in favor of nonalignment are to be believed; economic problems could be tackled on their merits, outside the special political aims usually implied in bilateral aid and without fear of wounding sensibilities or seeming to intervene. UN intervention seems to be more legitimate and acceptable than national measures of this kind.

American aid ought to be largely multilateralized, in order to avoid the need for constant—and inconsistently implemented—choices regarding who ought to receive what kind of aid and in order to stimulate recipient participation in the planning of aid measures. Availability of UN aid funds should be multiplied, perhaps, by a factor of 10 over current resources; more if other donor nations follow the American lead. Ampler funds will allow the mounting of more and different kinds of aid projects, permit fuller evaluation of results, and finance additional training facilities. They will also permit the UN to devote more human resources to the supervision of projects. Most specifically, the funds will make possible the creation of large corps of career UN aid supervisors and administrators in expanded and specially trained groups of resident representatives and deputy resident representatives.

A coordinated approach implies the reduction of American support to social and economic activities in the specialized agencies that do not qualify. It also requires that the United States and all other industrialized nations engage in serious soul-searching, to determine whether their trade policies aid or hinder the economic development of the Third World. It may turn out that the GATT approach remains relevant to trade among industrial countries, whereas a different set of rules ought to be worked out for trade among developing nations and between them and the industrialized world. Moreover, since the trade among industrial nations accounts for so much of total world trade, special rules departing from the principles of equal, competitive, and nondiscriminatory treatment must sometimes be observed even in trade among industrial nations. Special rules are particularly necessary for the introduction of new products competing with the exports of Third-World nations. Trade rules geared to development needs thus require some kind of planning, a periodic survey of what ought, or ought not, to be done along purely commercial lines. A coordinated approach also calls for new institutional devices such as special preferences and commodity agreements that may be actually uneconomic from the Western viewpoint. It calls for easier credit terms and new kinds of credit to finance more uneconomic projects. It calls for a world monetary policy that respects development aspirations in addition to the payments and liquidity needs of the West. *Above all, it involves a consciousness of the possible effects of innovation on the earning and growth capacity of the poor two-thirds of the world, a subordination of further economic growth in the North to the desirability of letting the South catch up.* We ought to be ready to tolerate an untidy world-trading system, the growth of many new common markets and free trade areas that derogate from GATT principles and fail to meet the stringent criteria of the optimal economic growth doctrine. We are well launched toward such a "system" anyway. Finally, the institutionalized confrontation between rich and poor—in UNCTAD and similar organs—is a fact of life basic to a coordinated and rationalized approach to aid and trade.

Placing UNCTAD in this position implies several very major institutional innovations. It means that the principle of majority voting must be abandoned wherever it may be permitted constitutionally. Since the first sharp splits at the 1964 conference, UNCTAD wisely makes all decisions by "consensus" and "conciliation"; that is, votes may be taken in each of the caucuses, but global policies are negotiated until general agreement is reached. Thus voting is avoided in plenary meetings. This procedure ought to be the general rule in all UN aid and trade bodies. Majoritarianism makes no sense at all when some twenty-five countries provide the aid and markets for about one hundred other countries. But UNCTAD, in turn, will reflect the economic regionalization of the world in that it will be animated by the three major regional organizations: OECD representing the industrial West, COMECON the industrialized Communist nations, and the sprawling Group of the 77 the Third World. Conciliation and consensus negotiations, in short, will take shape in the interplay between these three power centers of real economic influence.

The principle of sovereign autonomy for specialized agencies, the UN Development Program, and the UN Industrial Development Organization must go; so must the separate status of a half-dozen small planning and forecasting bodies. All these bodies must become subordinate to a centralized and coordinated approach to trade and aid. The capacity of the social sciences to spot and project the destabilizing as well as the beneficial aspects of innovations must be included in the over-all planning system. Hence UNCTAD must be advised by a UN Social Planning Board. But UNCTAD should become the sovereign agency for negotiating trade, aid, and money matters, to which the UN Development Program, the IMF, and the IBRD should be entirely subordinate. The existing specialized agencies, finally, would merely remain as dependent executing agencies of the UNDP.

5

The Next Challenge:
Human Rights, Science, and Technology

Peacekeeping, alliances, international grants, and technical aid have made up the bulk of international life since 1948. They have dominated the work of international organizations and preoccupied their members. Yet, even before the advent of the multipolar system with its heterosymmetrical distribution of power, three other issues arose: decolonization, international protection of human rights, and the global use of science. Although the issues are less prominent than military and economic objectives of nations, they are increasingly important to aspirations of the Third World; and the Third World, in turn, more aggressively makes its demands known in the emerging multibloc system. In American eyes, the future pattern of enmeshment becomes controversial and perhaps undesirable as the demands of the Third World grow more intense and as the issues of human rights and colonialism are increasingly experienced as social unrest and change *within the United States*. Domestic racial tension and international enmeshment become linked. Science generates new controversy as the United States desires more strands of scientific interdependence, to regulate exploration of the ocean bottom, safety in space, or environmental pollution; but at the same time, we fear the implications of science as they cause more social unrest at home and abroad through automation and the advance of synthetics.

PROGRESSIVE ENMESHMENT AND HUMAN RIGHTS

American policy in the UN with regard to the international protection of human rights was largely propagandistic in style and anticommunist in substance during the bipolar period. Like all other member nations, the

United States voted for the Universal Declaration of Human Rights in 1948 and thus endorsed a set of norms with great moral resonance but no legal force. At the same time, the United States made great use of UN organs to accuse Communist regimes of violations of human rights and to demand UN censure of such acts. As one result of these charges, ILO adopted the two comprehensive conventions dealing with freedom of association and the right to collective bargaining, texts the United States hoped to be able to use at Soviet expense. For similar reasons, the United States supported a number of treaties that presented ratifying states with specific obligations to prevent and punish violations of rights. The convention outlawing genocide is the most prominent. But when it came to providing teeth for these arrangements, the United States balked. Instead of legally binding commitments, conciliation commissions, judicial proceedings, and public debates, the United States preferred technical assistance to countries that would try to protect the human rights of their people.

Nor was the United States very happy with the effort launched by the UN to translate the Universal Declaration into a legally binding covenant. One issue was the question of whether "human rights" were essentially the political rights associated with the practice of democracy—the American position—or whether they included substantive matters such as the right to a job, a family, education in one's own language, full employment, and social security—the position argued by the Soviet bloc and developing nations. The United States tended to regard these substantive economic and social policies as the product of the exercise of political rights rather than as fundamental legal norms. Further, the Soviet bloc wished to limit the enjoyment of all rights by subjecting them to the need for public order and state policy. Another issue involved the question of whether there is a "collective" right to self-determination and to the control over natural resources, a question answered negatively by the United States. Finally, how could human rights, even if defined to everyone's satisfaction, be implemented or enforced under UN control? As the debate in the General Assembly increasingly veered toward specific formulations opposed by the United States, the earlier enthusiasm for the covenant began to pale.

American fear of enmeshment was not alleviated by the decision of the Assembly to draft two covenants, one dealing with political and civil rights subject to regular reporting, investigation, and conciliation of complaints of violations, and one dealing with the more controversial economic, social, and cultural rights, which would merely set standards for future attainment by member states. The two texts were completed and adopted by a unanimous General Assembly in December of 1966. But the United States' affirmative vote contained no hint of a willingness to ratify the covenants. The United States was particularly reluctant to commit itself to any international obligations that were justiciable under the aegis of the ICJ. It became a party to the Court's Statute only with the reservation that the compulsory jurisdiction of the ICJ over the United States excluded "disputes with regard to matters which are essentially within the domestic jurisdiction of the United States of America as determined by the United States of America." [1]

[1] This is the famous "Connally Reservation." U.N. Treaty Series, I, pp. 9-13.

Even though the domestic attitudes toward the international protection of human rights had not markedly changed by 1961, the Kennedy Administration decided to adopt a more aggressively favorable position on advancing the cause. In thus deciding to project a pro-Third-World image to the international community, the Administration was actually bowing with good grace to the very same force to which the outgoing Eisenhower Administration had adjusted more grudgingly. In addition, of course, the Kennedy Administration was also pleasing American civil rights advocates who had been less successful in gaining President Eisenhower's attention. And since hatred of all forms of racial discrimination and colonialism had acquired the proportions of a typhoon, the Kennedy Administration chose to throw in its lot wholeheartedly with the emerging world forces—up to a point. The limit to America's enthusiasm for a UN role in human rights protection turned out to be the matter of collective rights and the continued distrust of conventions.

Washington "embarked on a new policy of considering UN human rights conventions on their merits . . . [they] can play a vital role in defining standards, clarifying experiences, and exposing to the consciences of the world denial of what should be the heritage of all," said a government spokesman.[2] He explained that American adoption of human rights conventions would stress the interdependence between the enjoyment of liberties and the maintenance of peace, and it would encourage other nations to ratify the conventions. Conversely, the United States would be able to criticize honestly states that violate norms they have accepted, and the American view of the conventions would be given more weight than heretofore. Even though the Administration then asked Senate advice and consent for the ratification of the UN Conventions on Political Rights of Women and Genocide and ILO Convention on Forced Labor (none of which would have had the effect of changing domestic law), the Senate took no action.

Nor did the Johnson Adminstration's enthusiasm last very long. By 1964 its UN spokesman noted that with the completion of decolonization, new nations seemed to lose interest in the protection of human rights as they proceeded to suppress those of their own citizens who dissented. Economic development was given primacy over the right to speak, vote, or write freely; ethnic and national aggregates were considered the beneficiaries of UN-defined rights, not individual men. American disapproval of the trend in the UN was expressed by Arthur Goldberg when he urged that "the ultimate object of UN activities, the ultimate object of any organized society, domestically or internationally, is man—the individual."[3]

The single human right to which the UN majority has remained passionately devoted is freedom from racial discrimination. The UN in 1965 adopted a strongly worded convention outlawing all forms of racial discrimination. UNESCO in 1960 had adopted an equally sweeping conven-

---

[2] Richard N. Gardner, in *Department of State Bulletin* (August 26, 1963), pp. 320-21.
[3] Arthur Goldberg, in *Department of State Bulletin* (Oct. 11, 1965), p. 586. Also *ibid.*, Nov. 30, 1964, pp. 787-89; Sept. 21, 1964, p. 418.

tion outlawing discrimination in education, following the ILO's adoption in 1958 of a similar text with respect to employment. The American voice on this issue, however, had barely been audible—except in joining the global catharsis of castigating South Africa. It was only after 1961 that American delegates urged that South African policy violated Article 56 of the UN Charter in not promoting the advancement of human rights. At first anxious merely to have the UN go on record in opposing *government policies* that permit or decree discrimination, the United States eventually accepted stronger language that castigates discriminatory measures irrespective of government complicity. Clearly it was no accident that the course of American race relations and tensions found its counterpart in a more forthright American policy in international councils.

But the fact remains that even after 1961 the establishment of international norms for human rights met with tepid enthusiasm in the United States. In supporting the UNESCO Convention, the United States delegate also announced that because of the federal government's limited powers over education, the United States would be unable to ratify the text. Efforts were made by the United States to weaken the UN Anti-Discrimination Convention by removing the provision that enjoins states to suppress groups and prosecute citizens advocating racial intolerance. American spokesmen argued that such suppression would be a violation of freedom of speech; upon failing to win their point, they—in praising the Convention—nevertheless declared that the article in question would not impose new obligations on the United States.

Of all the global agencies to which the United States belongs, UNESCO has probably been most closely intertwined with human rights. UNESCO's initial purposes—before it, along with other specialized agencies, was swallowed by Cold War politics—included the prevention of future war by inculcating respect for individual human rights, by combating the evolution of the antihuman doctrines epitomized by Nazism. This was to be achieved by means of education and information campaigns in which the services of *individual* intellectuals, private groups of humanitarians, and professionals, rather than governments, would be central. Consistent politicization of UNESCO shattered this approach, and the organization's program in favor of human rights is now formulated by its Director-General only with the permission of the member governments and the budgets voted by them. American policy has been vacillating and inconsistent with respect to the general UNESCO program, including its human rights component.

UNESCO's services are all in the realm of advice and technical assistance. To be effective, governments must permit the information to be circulated, and they must consent to the operations of UNESCO on their soil. Nevertheless, UNESCO has aroused more passionate opposition as an "unpatriotic" agency in the United States than it has anywhere else; conversely, it has also had more enthusiastic and emotional support from humanitarian and libertarian groups in the United States than it has had elsewhere—and these attitudes have remained constant for twenty years. Therefore, the State Department has made little use of UNESCO, preferring not to call attention to its existence. Before 1960, the United States generally opposed the program, counseled retrenchment, and proved uninterested in generous financial support. After 1960, however, America discovered the utility of UNESCO teacher-training services for advancing the nation-building program in Africa—the same program that was to be served with foreign aid strategically placed to foster self-confident, anticommunist regimes in former colonial territories. From that point on, American financial support for UNESCO suddenly increased without, however, yielding a discernible spurt of legitimacy in the mind of the American public. Nor is such a feeling likely to grow if the Convention on Discrimination in Education, through its enforcement machinery, were to be turned against practices in Mississippi or Alabama!

The key to the American malaise with the international protection of human rights, therefore, is the matter of enforcement and implementation. Until 1961, the United States had stressed the purely voluntary techniques of education, study, and technical assistance as the most appropriate for inducing nations to respect rights defined by the UN. And, indeed, the UN has considerably increased these activities. With the completion of the UN and UNESCO Conventions on Racial Discrimination, however, the mechanism for advancing implementation has become much more sophisticated and potentially enmeshing. The UN Convention provides for an 18-member Committee of Experts with the task of examining annual reports submitted by each party, describing efforts made to implement the convention; this committee submits its evaluations to the General Assembly. Governments may lodge complaints against each other, alleging violations of the convention, and the committee also has the task of examining and settling such complaints. Failing the agreement of the parties to these efforts, the committee can create a special conciliation commission to conduct additional inquiries and negotiate a solution. Should this solution be rejected, however, the committee is limited to using the power of publicity to bring about compliance. Finally, the convention creates a procedure whereby private individuals can lodge complaints against their own governments—provided the governments submit a special declaration accepting the jurisdiction of the committee to receive individual petitions. Some nations wanted to include an unconditional right of petition, and some wanted none at all. The United States supported the compromise actually chosen. The UNESCO Convention created a Conciliation and Good Offices Committee with very similar competences regarding the receiving and hearing of complaints, and with enforcement powers limited to issuing publicity adverse to the defaulting state, a procedure in use in the ILO since 1951. This time the United States, by abstention, declined to support the special protocol, thus confirming its malaise.

But the United States has endorsed the enlargement of the obligation of states to report annually to the UN and expressed its support for the creation of a standing UN machinery for giving greater effect to the Universal Declaration of Human Rights, possibly through the creation of a UN High Commissioner for Human Rights. Such an official could conciliate disputes over human rights in a setting in which the governments are determined to avoid the formal legal procedure associated with the ICJ. The High Commissioner could hear complaints, remind the parties of their obligations, suggest compromises, and use his prestige to enable pairs of governments to extricate themselves honorably from stalemated positions. Still, neither the United States nor the great majority of other countries have shown any interest in strengthening institutions capable of binding legal definition and enforcement. And the trend toward a multibloc world with widely divergent political and social values is unlikely to contribute to a growing willingness to submit disputes over the rights of one's own citizens to the compulsory adjudication of an international court. And so the United States prefers voluntary action; but she is accommodating herself to compulsory reporting and conciliation just the same, even though the bulk of the public hardly sympathizes. And circumstances may even propel her into a still more active role when larger foreign policy issues seem involved.

This possibility is illustrated by the unplanned and unwished evolution of the Inter-American Commission on Human Rights of the OAS. The United States did indeed favor policies strengthening democracy in the Western Hemisphere and opposing dictatorial regimes of the right and the left. These commitments, however, did not imply the desire to intervene, change policy, cut off aid, or withhold recognition every time an undemocratic change of government occurred; nor did they include a strong wish for a standing investigating body, able to pinpoint violations of rights that interfere with the practice of democracy. Yet, just such a body evolved after 1960, in indirect response to certain reformist Latin-American regimes' demands for collective intervention on behalf of democracy. At the same time, an Inter-American Court on Human Rights was to be created, but it died on the vine. The commission, composed of seven experts serving as private individuals, was to assist in "furthering respect" for human rights, thus providing a sop for the reformers, though not asserting itself otherwise. But it did assert itself, "despite early United States efforts to emasculate it." [4] Even though instructed to undertake only general studies and promotional activities, the commission nevertheless received and considered complaints alleging specific violations of rights by Latin-American governments. Furthermore, the commission interpreted its restrictive official mandate to allow on-the-spot investigations of the complaints, with the permission of the government concerned. Investigations have been carried out in the Dominican Republic, and complaints from several other Caribbean nations have been scrutinized. Further, the United States made its peace with the commission when it demonstrated its usefulness to American objectives in easing the transition to Trujillo's successors, observing the Dominican elections of 1963, energetically and successfully advancing respect for human rights in the Dominican civil war of 1965, as well as castigating Castro's Cuba. At the same time, the commission had the restraint not to force its services on anyone and to avoid the race discrimination issue in the United States. But it emerged as an autonomous body whose active role was legally recognized in 1966, an enmeshment resulting from an earlier vague commitment and an initial propagandistic motive. It could happen in the UN as well.

[4] Slater, *The OAS and United States Foreign Policy*, p. 256 ff.

PROGRESSIVE ENMESHMENT AND DECOLONIZATION

"We should be eternally grateful to the UN," said an Undersecretary of State, "that the complex business of transforming half a hundred new states from dependence to sovereignty has, for the most part, been accompanied by speeches rather than by shooting." He thought this good for world peace because it hastened the end of colonialism, even though it also resulted in the "premature" addition to the UN of many "ill-prepared nations." [5] The desire to accelerate the demise of a practice that was bound to embitter future relations between the numerically growing Third World —enthusiastically supported by the Soviet bloc—caused the United States to join the anticolonial bloc. This policy, however, came to an end when the implications seemed to be nation-building at the expense of values cherished by the United States. And it took shape only after an earlier policy of indifference was challenged by the Third World.

Under the UN Charter the responsibilities and institutional enmeshments of colonial powers were modest enough. Colonies could be placed voluntarily under the trusteeship system. The trustee nation assumed the obligation to prepare the trust for "self-government or independence" without being bound to a timetable, and to give the needs of the indigenous population priority in its administration of the economy and society of the trust. Further, the trustee was obligated to report to the UN Trusteeship Council, permit inhabitants to petition the Council and to admit visiting UN missions instructed to inspect the implementation of the trust agreement. In fact, only 12 territories—all seized from enemy states in the two world wars—were placed under the system, and by 1968 all but three island groups in the Pacific had achieved independence or had been merged with neighboring independent states. American diplomacy had worked hard for this formula in 1945. It legitimated the take-over from Japan of the Micronesian island groups and their transformation into a "strategic" United States trust territory in which military preparations and tests were permitted on sites immune from UN inspection or supervision.

For all other colonial territories, the colonial powers bound themselves to give priority to the needs and well-being of the indigenous inhabitants and to take all measures to advance them toward "self-government," *not* independence. Further, they agreed to report annually to the UN on their policies in each territory under their sovereignty, but they did not have to report on political matters. The United States thus acquired responsibility to account for its stewardship in Puerto Rico, Samoa, Guam, and the Virgin Islands.

The obligation to report annually was soon escalated into a major measure of international control, ending in 1961 with the *de facto* merger of the two procedures: The Special Committee on the Situation with Regard to the Implementation of the Declaration on the Granting of Independence to Colonial Countries and Peoples (commonly known as the Committee of

[5] George Ball, "The United Nations Today," *Department of State Bulletin* (Nov. 16, 1964), pp. 695, 698.

Twenty-Four) assumed the power to tell each colonial nation *when* to set a territory free, to *whom* the free government is to be turned over, and *how* the transfer is to be made. It also assumed the power to visit colonies, hear petitioners, negotiate with colonial administrators, conduct plebiscites, and recommend condemnations of colonial powers to the parent General Assembly. Clearly, the political and legal power of the UN in the field of decolonization had grown immensely in fifteen years. Could the United States be sure that its freedom of action would remain unimpaired?

American policy accommodated itself to this institutional web only because it was difficult to resist the Third-World argument that self-determination, the *collective* self-determination of territorial groups, was the supreme human right on which all other rights depended. Decolonization, the protection of human rights, and the fight in favor of "freedom" became one syndrome in which the anticommunist crusaders' stance of the United States had to accept the interpretation of the Third World if Africa and Asia were to remain nonaligned or allied to the West. And so the United States reluctantly accepted a constantly growing role of the Trusteeship Council with its powers of supervising colonial administration and the creation of independent states. We accepted the right of the General Assembly to determine when the obligation to report on administration in non-self-governing territories can be terminated. And we reluctantly joined the Third World in holding that Portugal and South Africa were violating human rights, stifling self-determination, and threatening world peace by their racial policies within their own territories. But we opposed coercive measures against them. In 1960 we abstained when a near-unanimous General Assembly called for a "speedy and unconditional end to colonialism in all its forms and manifestations." [6]

Still, the controversy over the meaning of the right to "self-determination" and its many substantive and procedural implications caused the United States great difficulty. The inclusion of this right in the two covenants on human rights (see p. 85) was one of the reasons for American coolness toward the texts; the subsidiary right of permanent national sovereignty over natural resources brought to the fore the tangled issues of foreign investment, the role of private enterprise in economic development, and the right of new nations to nationalize foreign-owned mines and oil wells. American spokesmen sought unsuccessfully to resolve the issue by having the UN define the right to self-determination in a general legal formula protecting the *individual*, rather than a *collective* political right useful to the Third World in the general struggle for decolonization, territorial and economic. But the persuasive power of numbers asserted itself by 1958 and 1959: even though the United States opposed the highly emotional and politicized approach to the question of self-determination, she consented to serve on UN commissions charged with surveying alleged violations of that right.

Much ambivalence was evident when the United States had to adjust to the Assembly's revolutionary declaration. In part because of American insistence that the admitted right to self-determination need not necessarily

[6] General Assembly, Resolution 1514 (XV) on Granting of Independence to Colonial Countries and Peoples, Dec. 14, 1960, par. 1.

lead to full independence, the United States abstained on the crucial vote. Other reasons for such self-effacement were that the resolution did not recognize the need for a socioeconomic base for political stability and the right of the administering power to maintain law and order. Nevertheless, after it was passed, the Special Committee created to implement the resolution was endorsed by the U.S. delegate, who said:

> We believe its main function should be to survey the situation and to present to the Assembly . . . guiding principles of action in the all-important area.[7]

Such adaptive powers proved to be insufficient, because the Committee of Twenty-Four promptly interpreted its mandate to be far more active and specific. The principle of parity of representation was abandoned when the committee was stacked with Third World representatives. It heard petitioners, investigated complaints, visited most colonial territories, and gave the colonial powers instructions about which of several rival nationalist groups should be made the government when "immediate" independence arrived. The United States gradually joined the outvoted minority of Western nations on the committee in opposing the dramatic tactics of the majority that pressed for immediate withdrawal of the administering power and urged that the most radical nationalist group become the successor. In fact, the propensity of the majority to invest only neutralist or Communist-leaning groups with UN legitimacy proved to be the feature that made the work of the committee unpalatable to Washington. As the Committee of Twenty-Four, for all practical purposes, became *the* organ to complete decolonization, the United States once more withdrew from the anticolonial consensus and rejoined the West.

How did the United States fare when its record as a colonial power was reviewed in the UN? Washington displayed increasing responsiveness to UN pressure as far as the administration of the Pacific Island Trust Territory is concerned. The islanders complained bitterly to the UN Trusteeship Council about radioactivity and destruction of homes and fishing grounds due to American nuclear tests in 1953. In response to UN pressure the United States paid damages and ceased to use the Trust Territory for testing purposes. The islanders also complained about land alienation, insufficient economic development, and the continuation of rule by the U.S. Navy. The Trusteeship Council and its visiting missions repeated the complaint, resulting in a sharply increased American commitment to an economic development plan for the islands, transfer of administrative authority to the Interior Department, cessation of land alienation, and stepped up social services. Even though the UN continues to press the United States to set a date for the full independence of the islands, we have responded by creating a special commission to query the islanders as to how they wish to exercise their right of self-determination. In the meantime a central legislature with restricted powers, the Congress of Micronesia, was set up, after a long period in which the UN criticized the United States for creating political institutions only at the local level.

The Committee of Twenty-Four also had occasion to survey American

[7] Jonathan Bingham, in *Department of State Bulletin* (Jan. 8, 1962), p. 72.

policy in Samoa and the Virgin Islands in 1965. The committee recommended to the Assembly that the United States be reprimanded for not responding to requests to hasten their independence, dismantle military installations, and admit UN visiting missions. Even though the antimilitary portions of the resolution were not adopted, for lack of a two-thirds majority, the remainder was. Understandably, the embrace of the Third World initiated in 1961 soon led to a considerable cooling of ardor. Institutional enmeshment, however, had taken place in the meantime. Will it survive the multipolar system, which spawned it, and outlive the end of the colonial system as a whole?

OPINION, POLICY, AND THE FUTURE OF HUMAN RIGHTS

Did American public opinion support the UN's human rights program? Will it support such measures in the future? Evidence of public sentiment on the human rights and decolonization questions, with a focus on UN authority and American adherence to it, is very scarce. When put in very general terms, of course, Americans feel constrained by their national ethos to espouse both programs. At the onset of the multipolar world system, around 65 per cent of the public expressed support for UN-conducted plebiscites to determine the wishes of colonial peoples. Enthusiasm on that score seemed to decline during the Congo crisis, most dramatically in the South. After 1963, the Kennedy and Johnson administrations were reluctant to enmesh the United States further in the network of legal commitments to examine domestic legislation, report findings, and submit problems to UN conciliation agencies. Certainly there is some relation between this hesitancy and the fear that the public would repudiate such steps.

Certain elite groups, however, were persistently in favor of American commitment to a UN human rights program. Their concern has remained essentially unaltered since the adoption of the Universal Declaration in 1948. Between 1945 and 1955 "one or more civic, religious, business, child welfare, women's, technical, legal, medical, criminology, professional, informational, and labor groups pressed vigorously for machinery to handle human rights communications and petitions, for the right of complaint by individuals or organizations, a judicial review body for complaints—even a UN attorney-general to examine violations—and were met over and over again by the combined opposition of the British, Soviet and U.S. governments." [8] The same groups and their vigorous lobbying were largely responsible for the continued American commitment to UN-supported refugee and children's aid programs, even though the government had been eager to curtail them. Time has done nothing to diminish the enthusiasm of these groups. In 1964 they organized a nationwide committee grouping 35 citizens' organizations, overwhelmingly of a religious character, to lobby in favor of the ratification of UN human rights texts and for strong measures against South Africa. Although the Department of State had catered to these groups by appointing Mrs. Eleanor Roosevelt as the United States delegate to the

[8] Hyde, *The United States and the United Nations: Promoting the Public Welfare*, p. 190.

UN Human Rights Commission (the body that drafted many of the human rights texts), it cannot be said that Washington proved responsive in more substantive ways.

Nor are these elite groups unopposed by other groups. Conservatives generally and some business organizations in particular have opposed UN human rights treaties because they fear that an irresponsible President might "use the treaty-making power to effect internal social changes" and thus introduce socialism through the back door.[9] Business was not attracted to the UN program, for understandable reasons, when the UN Covenants acquired their articles dealing with the nationalization of natural resources. Groups that identify strongly with states' rights and private enterprise therefore had always opposed the UN program, and they continue to do so. Others, however, did not take this position until the advent of America's racial crisis in the late 1950's. It was only at that point that they began to relate attitudes toward domestic issues with international commitments.

Still others, moreover, seem to be making their peace with a gradually evolving global concern with human rights. A task force of the Republican National Committee, in 1960, advised that the United States support independence movements everywhere and support the right of foreign nations to choose *any* system of government that survives a free election. And many officials in Washington, by the early Sixties, felt that the American world image would be unnecessarily tarnished by standing aside from the human rights movement. Noting that UN scrutiny of American practices was unlikely to reveal anything to the world that the wire services and television networks had not already made very well known, Harlan Cleveland urged that

> Americans need to consider whether, as the necessary price for shining the UN's searchlight on oppression elsewhere, they are prepared to have the UN turn its attention to the mote in our own eye.[10]

But by 1968, one suspects, as the size of the mote had grown, so had the price of mutual enmeshment.

The special conditions under which the UN human rights task has acquired whatever authority and legitimacy it possesses are about to be swallowed by time and history. As the trusteeship system becomes a victim of its own success and as the Committee of Twenty-Four runs out of territories to free, it is unlikely that the new states still struggling to become nations will entertain with much fervor such things as internationally guaranteed rights of ethnic minorities or UN antidiscrimination measures from which their own dissenting citizens might benefit. In short, the success of decolonization spells the failure of a consistently applied UN human rights program. Why then should the United States continue to follow the cautiously and inconsistently positive policy it has adopted since 1961?

Harlan Cleveland suggested one reason. A growing world law of human rights, better than mere political invocation and propaganda speeches in the General Assembly, would aid the American policy of buttressing

---

[9] John Foster Dulles, April 6, 1953, quoted in *ibid.*, p. 174.
[10] Harlan Cleveland, "The Evolution of Rising Responsibility," *International Organization* (Summer, 1965, p. 832).

individual rights in new nations and thus launch them on the way to democratic stability and legitimacy. Further, such a policy would continue to serve the Cold War strategy of embarrassing communist totalitarian nations. But to succeed, the policy must take the road already traveled by ILO's human rights machinery: propaganda must yield to law and standing institutions for conciliation and adjudication. The United States would have to commit itself to permanently legitimate and authoritative third-party intercession. Washington's complaint of violations of freedom of speech in Egypt, for example, may be answered by a Syrian complaint of racial discrimination in Alabama. There is little reason to suppose that this degree of legal enmeshment is desired simply in order to retain ideological leverage abroad.

The dedicated activities of pro-human rights groups in the United States have yet to demonstrate their ability to overcome the stubborn divergences in national habits and aspirations exposed tellingly by Marcel Slusny:

> The vocabulary used is the same but the words do not convey the same concepts. Using as an example only the concept of trade union freedom, we see that all the delegates at International Labor Conference meetings proclaim their adherence to this principle. But it is clear that we are . . . witnessing a dialogue among deaf men because the delegates of the western countries, above all the trade unionists, conceive of union as an organ to defend an occupation which must remain independent of the state and of the employers. However, the Spanish delegate, for example, defends a corporatist conception, while the representatives of the Soviet bloc countries . . . consider unions as transmission belts between the state . . . and the producers.[11]

The superimposition of these major doctrinal and national differences over the related issue of whether collective or individual human rights should be the object of UN intervention is unlikely to facilitate a speedy end to the debate over whether human rights should be advanced through technical assistance, seminars, and discussions, or legal texts, conciliation commissions, and adverse international publicity. If the political will to carry out human rights commitments does not keep up with the legal possibilities of doing so, the growth of a luxurious jungle of resolutions, declarations, conventions, annual reports and conciliation commissions is likely to make little difference. American objectives regarding democracy at home and abroad are not likely to gain from discussion in the UN, particularly if they are laced with Cold-War and antineutralist arguments.

WORLD SCIENCE AND TECHNOLOGY: DANGER OR BLESSING?

Diverse scientists, engineers, theologians, and revolutionaries usually manage to agree on one proposition: the combined effect of scientific thought and its application in technology has been the transformation of the world. Within the last three centuries, man's increasing ability to manipulate the

---

[11] Marcel Slusny, "Quelques Observations sur les systèmes de Protection Internationale des droits de l'homme," *Mélanges Offerts à Henri Rolin* (Paris: A. Pedone, 1964), pp. 393-94.

physical environment has made greater changes in life styles than have occurred in the previous million years of human evolution. Few believe that these changes have reached a plateau, since the sum of scientific knowledge seems to double every decade; all agree that the devotion to scientific and technological progress creates problems of adaptation, diffusion, and understanding.

> The scientific revolution is here to stay. . . . Indeed, it is only beginning. What we have seen in the past is as nothing compared to the future. We shall be found wanting if we do not plan with that thought in mind. Our success in achieving the objectives of creative evolution requires both an ever more vigorous effort in science and technology and an enormous improvement in techniques for integrating the products of science and technology into society.[12]

A committee of the U.S. House of Representatives admitted that more and more science is indeed necessary to cope with the products of earlier discovery, but "our success in the development of such new knowledge must be accompanied by careful and improved methods of putting that knowledge to work. Otherwise we may strangle in the coils of an unplanned, unwanted, but unstoppable technocracy."[13]

Basic to the conundrum is the Janus-faced nature of science itself: it is both an agent for the improvement of man's lot and the author of some of his most urgent problems, including war. Nevertheless, men have stressed by and large only the progressive and even utopian aspects of science and technology. In international politics they have geared it to economic development, social advancement, and, *mirabile dictu,* peace. Put differently, men have been content to seek the adaptation of societies and nations to the demands of science and technological innovation. It is only in the most recent decade that voices of fear and doubt have suggested that man cannot stand much more innovation, that science and technology should, perhaps, be tailored to man's measure. In international politics and in the halls of international organizations, this has meant a simultaneous and confusing commitment to the reliance on science and to its banishment back into the genie's lamp.

Before we can deal with the place of international organizations and American policy in this welter of conflicting questions and trends, a few definitions must be introduced. *Science,* or basic science, is man's inquiry into the physical and biological nature of the universe (including man himself) using a systematic mode of thought based on the philosophy of science and employing primarily empirical tools of research. *Technology* will be used here as a synonym for *applied science,* or application of results or lessons of scientific inquiry to the control of man's physical and biological environment through fields such as engineering, medicine, meteorology, agronomy, anthropology, and psychology. Clearly, applied science includes social science insofar as the abstract lessons of social inquiry are self-

12 Glenn T. Seaborg, quoted in U.S. House of Representatives, Committee on Science and Astronautics (89th Cong., 2nd Sess.), *Inquiries, Legislation, Policy Studies re Science and Technology: Review and Forecast* (Washington: Government Printing Office, 1966), p. 20.
13 *Ibid.*

consciously related to policies designed to alter or control the environment, thus giving a certain apolitical, or transpolitical, twist to the making of public policy. Many physical and biological scientists, as well as psychologists and sociologists, claim that their recipes for social action are based on "science" rather than prejudice or crude self-interest and are therefore much superior to the hit-or-miss solutions devised by politicians. Marxists and many non-Marxists devoted to "peace research" maintain they possess a scientific basis for social decisions. The rigorous subordination of policy-making to such prescriptions is offered as the way to end the international conflict and diplomacy described in preceding chapters: it would substitute a different kind of knowledge for the interest-tainted consciousness of political actors. Are these claims justified?

We must thus deal with these questions: (1) When and how does basic science pertain to international relations? Does the diffusion of scientific knowledge contribute to peace, thus making international scientific cooperation a natural part of UN activity? (2) When and how does applied science or technology relate to international politics? How do international organizations get involved in dealing with the dangers of applied science or in advancing its benefits? (3) How has applied social science impinged on international politics? Do international organizations make use of applied social science rather than interest-dominated policy inputs? And at all times, of course, our concern remains the extent of American enmeshment in the web of scientific and technological interdependence, the witting or un-witting role of American policy in fashioning that web.

INTERNATIONAL ORGANIZATION
AND THE COMMUNITY OF SCIENCE

Basic scientific research, for all its prestige and for all the devotion of its practitioners, remains marginal to action at the intergovernmental level. UNESCO, the main agency with jurisdiction, confined its efforts to calling conferences and symposia designed to increase and accelerate the diffusion of basic scientific knowledge, to help in the formation of international associations of scientists, to call attention to problem areas in research sub-sequently dealt with by other means.

Although nations continue to dominate international cooperation in basic scientific research, scientists strongly resemble a "community" of their own. Thus their crucial role in policy-making deserves emphasis. Scientific research and the application of science to man's life are politically unique in that there is almost no public or elite opinion to influence policy; there prevails a vague but benign attitude of somehow considering all science "good." Lay government officials are usually unable to evaluate the nature and implications of scientific discoveries; they depend on science advisers and administrators in making decisions. In a very real sense, therefore, scientists working in or near government *are* the makers of national and international policy in their fields. What kind of people are they?

It is hardly surprising that scientists tend to transfer their character-istic mode of thought and analysis to social issues and public policy. Hence many of them think of national and international politics as straightforward problem-solving techniques, which lead them to naïve utopianism—or to its opposite, naïve belligerency. Instead of dealing with issues incrementally, they tend to "deal with the whole problem," usually conceived in politically naïve terms. Similarly, they prefer quantum jumps in knowledge to incremental improvements, and they question the intelligence of political leaders unable to deal with the human environment in such total terms. While some scientists tend to assert the value of technology for its own sake—to build the machine just because it is possible and interesting—others see their profession as serving mankind positively, as no profession has served it before, *provided* science can be confined to acts with exclusively peaceful consequences! When the obvious practice of international politics runs counter to these mental images, scientists are quick to portray themselves as peacemakers, as envoys of human understanding, as pure souls able to substitute the therapeutic powers of knowledge for the corrupting marsh of interest-dominated politics.

Hence the notion of a community of scientists, organized apart from government but in the service of international cooperation for peace, is a natural outgrowth of these ideas. The feeling gains strength from the mere numbers of scientists at annual international meetings: about 20,000 Americans met with 80,000 foreign colleagues at 2,000 conferences, colloquia, and seminars in the mid-Sixties. Some of the impulse for this burst of communication is inherent in the nature of basic research and reflects no political commitment. Equipment used in nuclear and high-energy physics research is beyond the capacity of most countries to acquire; therefore, the pooling of resources is necessary. Radio astronomy, space research, meteorology, and the exploration of the ocean floor are transnational by definition and, to be feasible, require cooperative arrangements. The explicit or implicit desire to use science to get "beyond politics" is also very pervasive.

The practice of scientific cooperation is thought to be helpful in this because it creates common interests and mutual trust. Research that is of interest to scientists anyway is clothed in the garb of an unwitting servant of peace: the needs of the research must lead to stronger international organizations with regulatory powers and the ability to stimulate more meetings, new international research centers, the systematic use of scientists in aiding economic development, disarmament, and therefore peace. Science is thought to produce political spin-offs because it is supremely rational, unvictimized by tradition and prejudice.

The International Council of Scientific Unions, with a membership of national scientific unions from 54 countries, is a powerful international lobby that has succeeded in inspiring, organizing, and carrying out some of the most impressive international cooperative research with the full financial support of governments, and with direct political results in some cases. Thus ICSU organized the International Geophysical Year and the exploration of the Antarctic Continent, leading directly to the Antarctic Treaty, neutralizing and demilitarizing that last body of land not yet annexed to some nation's sovereign impulse, preserving it for collaborative scientific exploration. A similar effort was the International Indian Ocean Expedition and the International Year of the Quiet Sun. Further joint forays into the natural sciences are planned. One is the continuous observation of the world's weather, in an effort to make total environmental forecasts; this aim has led to the establishment of the World Weather Watch under the auspices of World Meteorological Organization. The special radio communication systems required by the weather research satellites have resulted in increased powers of wavelength allocation for the International Telecommunications Union. Rising interest in joint basic biological and medical research—with the cure of cancer the ultimate goal—has given WHO new funds and tasks.

All its activities, committed to the search of knowledge, are based on the implicit assumption that all mankind will benefit from the results. Hence none of them have been politically controversial. The accrual of new powers to international organizations and scientific associations was readily accepted by governments, even actually lauded by American policy-makers. They too thought that cooperation among scientists and engineers under government auspices would yield a dedication to common needs and shared technical tasks to which even ideologically opposing nations could subscribe, thus building bridges to Communist and Third-World nations and fostering new international law and institutions. These sentiments continue to be expressed by the highest American leadership today.

But governments did not necessarily support international basic science for the pure and disinterested reasons that scientists like to stress. Governments expected to gain prestige, propaganda victories, and influence over foreign scientists while helping to attain purely scientific objectives. Indeed, the fact that political and transpolitical objectives are rarely irreconcilable in actual operations has not yet been grasped by many scientists. When a government is convinced that it will lose by participating in such an enterprise it will withdraw, as Peking China withdrew from the International Geophysical Year. Communist scientists have frequently attempted to use scientific conferences as media for passing resolutions critical of American foreign and military policy; four professional meetings held on Soviet soil in 1966 were marred by the intrusion of Cold-War politics. Nor have American scientists shown much resistance to making use of their gatherings for political purposes in which the search for rationality and sober judgment was not always evident. In short, the flowering of noncontroversial international basic science ventures under the auspices of the community of researchers has yet to demonstrate a uniform, even growth of rational problem-solving behavior in the realm of politics.

Nor has there been marked evidence of the progressive enmeshment of nations in collective enterprises of basic science, despite the lip service of governments. Organizations like ITU, WMO, WHO lack even the limited impact of the UN economic agencies. They simply regulate a well-defined area of undisputed and absolute interdependence of no significance to peace, or they collect and disseminate scientific knowledge discovered by national and private agencies. They do not evaluate ongoing or new basic research and judge its relevance to the future of science or to potential international systems of interdependence. It is only in the field of applied science that this threshold is being approached.

APPLIED SCIENCE AND INTERNATIONAL ORGANIZATION

Interest shown after 1953 in the international implications of science and technology was directly related to military considerations and to the Cold War. Growing involvement in scientific ventures at the UN level did *not* owe its birth to curiosity about the ocean floor, cosmic rays, quasars, or the earth's crust: it was conceived by fears of military insecurity.

The lead was assumed by the United States, which proposed that the peaceful use of nuclear energy be linked with stopping the proliferation of national nuclear programs having warlike implications. The mechanism was the International Atomic Energy Agency (IAEA), with the combined task of encouraging peaceful use of nuclear energy and providing international safeguards against the diversion of fissionable materials to war production. IAEA did not come into existence until 1957. It did not acquire powers commensurate with the American objective until the United States itself changed its policy in 1962. Further, the Soviet Union apparently did not decide to upgrade IAEA powers until the Russian leaders also acquired a vested interest in preventing nuclear proliferation. In addition, continued nuclear testing by the superpowers in the mid-Fifties prompted the General Assembly to denounce the hazards of fallout and radiation and to appoint a panel of experts to publicize the dangers of testing. Even though the United States was far from pleased with this interest in matters scientific, the fear generated by these efforts provided a further motive for internationalizing the militarily and politically embarrassing aspects of the atom. How the fear of the atom and efforts at nuclear arms control are linked to American policy on disarmament was discussed in an earlier chapter. By 1967 the initial desire to slow down the acquisition of military nuclear lore by less developed nations had resulted in voluntary American submission to IAEA inspection of national and bilateral reactor programs. Further, the superpowers want the IAEA to inspect compliance with the nuclear nonproliferation treaty. And in the process, a UN agency has become an important actor in the application of nuclear energy to national development programs.

Much the same impulse was at work in another field of applied science: the penetration of outer space. Characteristically, it is the technologically leading nation that first seeks to create international rules and procedures governing future research, in order to retain its lead and slow down the race. In the nuclear field, the United States was the leader; in the space race, it was the Soviet Union. Hence the Soviets took an early lead in seeking UN-sanctioned rules reserving space for peaceful purposes and barring its use for surveillance satellites. Furthermore, the Soviets wanted no private corporations engaged in space communications, whereas the United States insisted on the rights of private companies to participate in the creation of global communications systems. At the beginning of the Space Age, the United States was content to work for UN rules that would safeguard the right of all nations to launch probes and assure the security of astronauts and space vehicles. Hence agreement was reached on safety rules, on the permanent neutrality of celestial bodies, and on the rights of all nations to explore them. By the mid-Sixties the apparent stability of the balance of terror had led to a further agreement barring the placement of orbiting weapons in space. And all nations agreed to register their launchings with the UN, exchange scientific data, and to place a few of their scientific exploration efforts under the auspices of a UN launching site in India. But the United States persisted in its preference for unregulated national efforts using orbiting laboratories and satellites of military value and denied the UN a major role in space communications.

This American policy is being challenged by some scientists and other specialists, though it is not questioned by the public. Noting the unwillingness of the United States and other countries to forego expected military and commercial advantages from space research, some critics advocate that internationalization and demilitarization of the field be combined with a sharing of expected benefits, thus paying the less-developed countries for not establishing a military capacity in space. UN operation of communications satellites is suggested by those who fear the use of space for unregulated propaganda. Many other forms of international cooperation are suggested by scientists anxious to use the frontiers of knowledge beyond the stratosphere as a demonstration of peaceful UN activity and to publicize the feasibility of UN-conducted disarmament inspection. In the absence of actual American moves in this direction, the oft-repeated assurance that only international exploration makes sense does not sound very convincing.

So far at least, the main thrust toward more international interest in applied science developed from concern over rapid economic and social development. The advent of the Third World and the need felt by the industrial nations to meet more of its demands proved to be the crucial political stimulant to a different approach. Some early projects included coordinated international research on the properties of arid lands, desalination techniques, and massive research commitments on the part of IAEA to discover whether nuclear or conventional power sources are most appropriate for desalination plants.

The breakthrough in relating science to economic development, however, came in 1960. In that year the General Assembly went on record as instructing the Secretary-General to do everything in his power to advance the application of science and technology to human betterment. As early as 1956 the Assembly had prodded the Secretariat to survey all efforts then under way to hasten industrialization; two years later it instructed UNESCO to make a similar survey of the natural sciences, resulting in the adoption by 1961 of a ten-year applied science program by UNESCO and the recommendation that the UN create a new specialized agency devoted only to marshalling science for economic development. The Secretary-General implemented his new mandate in 1962 by convoking the giant UN Conference on the Application of Science and Technology to Development (UNCAST).

The work of the conference and the optimism with which Secretary General U Thant greeted it can be described only as "Science Rampant." There was some recognition that even though science and technology were considered benign agents of wholesome social change, their application in non-Western countries need not imply the wholesale imitation of the giant Western industrial-urban-scientific complex. In fact, the adaptation should be sensitive to what the local culture can and will bear without destroying itself in the process of modernizing. But such restraint was not shown in other areas of concern. The main need was said to be more scientists, and crash programs for training scientific personnel in all fields were featured to increase their numbers. Another central need was the multiplication of research and research training sites, as well as the more efficient diffusion of scientific information. Training and diffusion are to be accelerated through the construction of regional science centers in the Third World, in which all fields of science and technology will be brought to bear on the creation of a new class of scientists and their subsequent employment in systematic national development programs drawing on new knowledge in oceanography, meteorology, hydrology, agronomy, and demography.

Who is to do all this? UNCAST rejected the idea of a new specialized agency and thought of UNESCO as the primary agent of the work, as well as of the existing UN regional commissions. There was little evidence that much thought was given to which governments, because of their financial position, would be crucial in directing the process. Few delegates realized that "planning" involves more than a listing of scientific fields that are short of manpower. In fact, the only major institutional step taken as a consequence of the conference was the creation of the UN Advisory Committee on the Application of Science and Technology to Development, a group of eminent scientists serving as individuals. In 1965 the Committee established eight priority targets to be attacked internationally: food supplies, health, population, natural resources, industrialization, housing and urban planning, transportation, and new educational techniques especially suited for developing countries. They also specified potential research breakthrough areas useful in dealing with each of these, such as improvement of water resources or weather control. In 1966, the committee published a "World Plan of Action," a "planned international campaign to strengthen existing programmes and to add appropriate new arrangements to round out the total effort.[14] Specifically, the plan calls for massive manpower training programs and institution-building, more diffusion of technical knowledge linked to policies designed to make people accept innovation more readily, and the reorientation of scientific research toward meeting the special needs of developing nations. The number and kind of regional research and training centers are discussed, and 2,000 annual training fellowships are demanded. Science Rampant it is, with the undiminished optimism that this gigantic effort will automatically improve the lot of mankind and thereby contribute more or less directly to world peace. But so far, at least, the effort remains largely on paper, with each agency and each government continuing to follow development policies previously determined without the benefit of the "planning" of science and technology. Still, the area of applied science has not, so far, linked the United States to a chain of international commitments and obligations. The financial outlay devoted to these efforts is minimal compared to the funds devoted to the UN economic agencies. None of the specialized agencies or advisory committees has come close to acquiring powers of direction or control, though American diplomats have sometimes

[14] Economic and Social Council, *Official Records*, 41st Sess. 1966, Suppl. No. 10 (E/4206) par. 129.

proposed such a role. Finally, as long as the belief persists that any and all aspects of applied science are good for peace and welfare, the mere proliferation of unrelated activities defies control and direction. Enmeshment becomes an issue only when men realize that not all science is benign, that the application of science to agronomy can undo its application to rural development. When "planning" becomes more than a euphemism for strengthening the national research potential of new countries, when it is an international effort to coordinate and direct conflicting, diffuse aspects of scientific inquiry, the web of scientific interdependence will be woven more tightly. How far has applied social science gone in approaching this condition?

APPLIED SOCIAL SCIENCE AND INTERNATIONAL POLITICS

Sociologists and psychologists, particularly, but many others in applied social sciences and the natural sciences, think of their knowledge as transpolitical, offering solutions to tensions, hatreds, conflicts, and war—solutions that escape the political policy-makers who are concerned only with the articulation and defense of national interests. Some of them argue that these problems are caused by politicians in the first place. How then can the substitution of social science for politics be advanced by international organizations led and financed by politicians representing 130-odd national interests?

UNESCO's work in applied social science suggests an answer. Like other scientists, researchers associated with UNESCO believed that their findings could usefully be applied to specific social problems, notably prejudice, intergroup hostility, and war. Consequently, they undertook a series of activities loosely called the "tensions project," which prepared and distributed booklets describing various national ways of life. In addition, a four-country project compared the sources of intergroup tensions, and other conferences were held to discuss causes of tensions and wars. Finally, research was done on ethnocentrism, xenophobia, race prejudice, and the psychological causes of aggression. For the most part, these efforts were a failure, either because they did not add to existing knowledge or because the results were ignored by the world. In other cases "research projects proved to be too delicate politically to be pursued, failing an official invitation from a government to carry them on." [15] When the implications of the social issues submitted to research ran counter to government policy, the research was stopped. Conversely, UNESCO-sponsored training and research on the social implications of economic development have consistently grown and have prospered because governments are interested in the results. The very commitment to "peace" often cited by social scientists as basic to their work makes this activity suspect to governments unconvinced that their own interest in higher production, stable commodity prices, strong armies, or dedication to democracy has much to do with the links to peace seen by social scientists.

[15] UNESCO, *Appraisal of UNESCO's Programmes for the Economic and Social Council* (Paris, 1960), pp. 105-6.

Social problems are almost entirely infused with political values, whereas "problems" in the natural sciences are not so perceived at the moment. American policy has been particularly hostile to social science research under UN auspices allegedly related to world peace; Washington favors such a policy only when it is linked to the basic goal of urban reconstruction, advancing economic development, education, and the ability of a nation to plan its own future. Hence it is hardly surprising that the portion of the UNESCO budget devoted to applied social science has not exceeded 3 per cent. Only programs clearly related to economic development demonstrate their capacity to legitimate themselves.

When industrialization was the problem, the majority of nations in ECOSOC, as early as 1956, happily bestowed scientific credentials on the social practitioner. Demographic studies and population policy were recognized as important areas of concern. After many years during which certain member nations resolutely blocked WHO's role in birth control education, WHO became concerned with child welfare as well as with population pressure and control. Today, WHO is a pioneer in using systematic social science to forecast social and ethical side effects of medical change, so that implications of public health work may be determined. Other UN research institutes seek to determine how best to plan the social welfare of groups caught up in the throes of industrialization, how to match social with economic benefits. Systematic inquiries are also trying to find how to improve development aid programs, particularly their evaluation and administration. All these efforts recognized the importance of detached inquiry in policy-making; but they remain piecemeal and uncoordinated. Nor were they inspired by any coherent notion of how industrialization, social change and contentment, scientific education and the spread of technology may interconnect to augment or destroy each other.

Perhaps for the first time there is underway in the UN now a political and intellectual process that aims at comprehensive and rational development planning, subordinating politics, and short-range interest to knowledge —or so it looks at first blush. The effort in question is the deliberate analysis now being undertaken to plan the Second Development Decade, to begin in 1970. It involves professional economists as well as UN administrators, representatives of the interests of specialized agencies and UN regional commissions, lobbyists for organizational vested interests, and expert economic planners interested only in an optimal allocation of global resources.

The centerpiece of this planning effort is the UN Programming and Projection Center; there the world growth model that is to guide the allocation of organizational programs and resources is taking shape. The center's recommendations are then submitted for discussion to the UN Committee for Development Planning, a group of eighteen experts serving as individuals, called into being by ECOSOC. The committee has the task of collecting and projecting all available information and techniques that lead to the efficient implementation of national development plans. But in its work the committee has developed criteria and techniques for *judging* such plans in the perspective of UN principles. It now has the additional task of shaping and submitting to ECOSOC a world development plan, and perhaps exercising some powers of control in implementing it after 1970.

Once the model is accepted, it will be important in deciding which specialized agency will undertake what program in the execution of the plan. It is already clear that FAO—which has produced a long-range indicative plan for world agricultural development—will adjust its agricultural and commodity policy accordingly and that ILO will prepare and seek to implement regional employment and manpower training programs that fit the plan. UNESCO's work in educational development will be dovetailed with the employment projections, and WHO's public health work will fit in with the population and urbanization projections.

But the model has not yet been accepted as an authoritative guide. It is being widely criticized for being overconcerned with economic variables, to the exclusion of the social and human dimensions, of asserting the virtues of economic development as self-evident without regard for the social and political transformations that may be engendered unwittingly. The member nations and ECOSOC have not yet spoken; UNCTAD's role as the spokesman for the developing nations is being asserted but not defined; OECD, as the agent of the financial contributors to the Decade, has gone its own way with its own projections. Planning the Second Development Decade is indeed a giant first step in the rational allocation of world skills, resources, and talents for control; but it surely has not demonstrated the unique qualities of governance claimed for science.

The link between basic and applied sciences, and their planned integration with the life of the international society, is complex. Planning can mean deliberate, self-conscious assignment of research and development priorities for the positive exploitation of the unknown on behalf of human welfare. But it can also mean the imaginative projection of unsettling and disturbing innovations, the avoidance of disruptive exploitation and its political consequences. If scientific advance is indeed inevitable it is as likely to lead to "national science" and to national self-assertion as it is to result in the peaceful internationalization of knowledge. *Conflict, indeed scientifically aggravated conflict, remains in the forefront of possibility— unless one of the unintended consequences of randomly applied science is the realization that it may be too dangerous to permit this process to continue without international regulation.*

Obviously, the world is far from this realization. International planning —to the extent that the various UN commissions and conferences can be said to engage in it—is confined to assigning priorities to the positive exploitation of knowledge, particularly economic development. Our final chapter suggests the kind of world unwilled enmeshment may produce, to correct—or aggravate—this condition.

6

The Future International System

The major and perhaps the sole justification for using systems theory in the discussion of international politics is its ability to link the will of governments with the shape of the world to come. It is policy that produces the "system," though the system then goes on to constrain future policy or to dictate its limits.

"Discussion of whether or not we should be in the United Nations is about as useful as discussion of whether or not we should have a United States Congress," comments Richard N. Gardner. He continues:

> What we really need is to accept the fact that international organizations are here to stay and to turn to the much more difficult question of how we can use them better to promote our national interest. We need to discuss the UN and other international organizations in operational rather than in symbolic terms. We need to consider in professional detail just what these agencies do and how they could do it better.[1]

Because of commitments here expressed, the multipolar hetero-symmetrical system of the current era resulted from the policies followed by governments in the previous tripolar era. Because of the persistence of these commitments, we assert that the policies followed by governments during the multipolar era will produce a new system we may label "multibloc asymmetrical."

Of course, the giant assumption we make here is that governments will simply follow the logic of the course sketched during the present system and expressed in Gardner's judgment, thus swimming with the tide already

[1] Gardner, *In Pursuit of World Order, op. cit.,* p. 6.

flowing. The system projected is what it is only because we now treat governments as the helpless victims of earlier decisions. This assumption may be wrong. Governments may deliberately refuse to float along with the current; and if they successfully assert themselves, they will be turning the tide or setting up a countercurrent. Indeed, such a choice may be desirable.

Our job first of all is the presentation of a scenario with probable future world trends *not* subject to easy human manipulation or social learning. Then we must describe the multibloc asymmetric system that will characterize international politics in such a setting, *provided* that present trends continue. Both analyses will then set the scene for the reader's own choice as to whether he wishes to let enmeshment take its ordained path or whether he wants the United States to strike out on a different road.

THE WORLD OF THE BASIC MULTIFOLD TREND

There can be little doubt that the world will be characterized for many decades to come by the "basic multifold trend." [2] This trend is made up of separate strands that are by no means mutually re-enforcing; perhaps the opposite will be the case. Nor are the items that make up the trend subject to any social learning that is now discernible. They just go on, as if of their own volition. Thus, culturally, the world will be more and more sensate, preoccupied with empirical perception, secular, humanistic, utilitarian, and hedonistic. People will be less and less willing to defer gratification; they will be bent exclusively on immediate enjoyment of whatever they value. Elites will tend toward both egalitarianism and meritocracy. Scientific knowledge of all kinds will accumulate even more rapidly than it does now. Society will change faster and more universally in proportion to the application of this scientific knowledge through technology and its diffusion. Industrialization will be worldwide, though its benefits may not be; both affluence and leisure will increase in proportion, but population will also continue to burgeon, thus giving us a continuing race between food supply and people. Primary occupations will decline even more in importance, and secondary occupations will begin a downward trend. Education and literacy will spread more evenly throughout the world, and so will the capability for mass destruction through war. Urbanization will reach the point of the megalopolis, if not the necropolis.

The major technical revolutions of the next twenty years will include a vast increase in computers, data retrieval, and their application, so that instantaneous factual information will be available to decision-makers on almost everything—but also to the increasingly literate and aware public. Developments in biology may result in control over heredity, motivation, and the length of human life. The oceans will be increasingly explored and exploited, and the weather will be subjected to manipulation. New forms of energy will be developed making man less dependent on coal and access to fresh water, with wide implications for location of industries. [3] Some of the

[2] Herman Kahn and Anthony J. Wiener, "The Next Thirty-Three Years: A Framework for Speculation," *Daedalus* (Summer, 1967), p. 706.

[3] This sketch is taken from Nigel Calder, ed., *The World in 1984* (Baltimore: Penguin Books, 1965), vol. 2, summaries after p. 190.

more obvious "social problems" associated with these trends—not necessarily capable of being solved by such learned behavior as forecasting and planning—include unemployment, status deprivation, and society's inability to assimilate an excess of educated, aspiring counterelites. The race for food will imply agrarian unrest, and the reliance on cybernetic equipment will lead toward the meritocratic rule of communications scientists and technicians. Since more work will be done by fewer people, private life will become crucial; the home and the "communal pad" will be new centers of activity.

The dominance of these trends is likely to result in the arrival of a society now often labeled postindustrial, almost certainly, it will come quite soon to the West and to Japan, and eventually to the successfully industrializing nations of Asia, Africa, and Latin America. The postindustrial society is characterized by very high per capita income, the dominance of tertiary and quaternary economic pursuits and by effective floors on welfare. New social aggregates, neither "public" nor "private," will be the major source of innovation; and as cybernation reigns supreme, the market will decline in decision-making importance. Since most institutions will become obsolete within a generation, "learning" will be a continuous activity in the sense of making people adapt to change beyond their rational control; quite literally, everybody will be going to school most of the time. Work-oriented and achievement-oriented values will disappear as the pursuits associated with a sensate culture predominate and all human group activity is legitimated as psychotherapy.

The role of government and foreign affairs in such a setting calls for a further comment. As accepted values erode, we can no longer expect a consensus on notions such as the "national interest"; perhaps the postindustrial nation will no longer be an object of value at all to its citizens. The government may become an agency taken for granted as the dispenser of largesse and physical security that one assumes to be his right. More and more people will be able to afford to behave as spoiled children, and American society could become a loose network of self-indulgent groups profoundly indifferent to the issues that make up this book. But someone would remain to feed and exploit the data banks, to design and deploy nonkilling but lethargy-inducing missiles, to plan the curricula for the next generation of adaptive gene selectors and ocean ranchers. The ruling meritocracy would inherit government by default.

Can this sort of widespread alienation survive? Chances are that the alienated would eventually seek to influence public decisions once more and develop appropriate ideologies. The mood of soma-centered withdrawal from public values—and the withdrawal from world affairs implicit in this mood—may then give rise to a new chiliasm of mission, reform, overthrow, and involvement. And the commitment-withdrawal-recommitment cycle of the American foreign policy mood might remain intact even in a postindustrial setting.[4] Nor should we forget that while the West is working itself toward the satiation of the postindustrial psyche, whole nations in the less developed world will continue to be ruled by genocide, famine, guerrilla brutality, and messianic behavior.

[4] Kahn and Wiener, op. cit.

All sorts of "problems" will abound twenty years hence, problems bequeathed to us by the pace of change associated with the basic multifold trend. We do not know whether these problems are amenable to solutions other than "progressive adjustment." We cannot tell whether man will have a consciousness of danger, of a need to forecast and to plan early corrective steps. We must suspect that technological and scientific innovation will go on growing exponentially. We must be dubious of man's ability to learn to mold these forces according to his hopes and fears. Thus we can affirm the tension between the Third World's desire to modernize and be rich and the West's ability to help, but we do not know whether the tension will result in a race war or a welfare world based on a regional economic division of labor. Will the erosion of national values in the West bring about similar disintegration in the Third World? In time to avert a race war? Will preoccupation with shaping man's physical environment make all international policies of the past obsolete? Will total ecological planning yield a new mentality for the ruling meritocracy in Malawi, as in Sweden, in Cambodia as in Czechoslovakia? Economic growth may lead to bitter disenchantment; the sensate life may spawn boredom and crime. Megalopolis may prove to be unbearable, and public order may come to depend on the regular administration of new and powerful tranquilizers. None of this is certain; all is possible. The minor troubles associated with questions such as who controls the weather, what agency decides on the eugenic balance of Upper Volta and Ecuador, and how this affects Uzbekistan and Montenegro seem quite bearable in comparison. So is the vexing question of whether the twenty new moderately industrial nations will soon have advanced weapons systems at their disposal, thus creating among themselves arms races and deterrence patterns of the kind familiar to the superpowers in 1969.[5]

This is the evolving setting of world politics. It will determine the future of the web of interdependence if existing trends are simply accepted by policy-makers and if systemic learning continues to take the form it has enjoyed for the last decade.

A MULTIBLOC ASYMMETRIC SYSTEM

The characteristics of the era in which we are living are changing before our very eyes. Alliances are visibly declining in cohesion and purpose. The ideological struggle between the superpowers is being muted. New nations declare themselves nonaligned almost as soon as their flags rise in front of the palace of the government, as the North–South issue predominates in their minds over the East–West confrontation more familiar to us. Economics and economic blocs are therefore more important than many military and ideological groupings. This trend is well underway and it rolls on whether willed or not by the United States. What kind of configuration can we predict for the international system if the trend continues unchecked?

We must exclude certain kinds of futures as incompatible with any now visible aspects of the multifold trend, at least for the next twenty to thirty years. There will be no world government based on voluntary federa-

[5] Calder, *The World in 1984, op. cit.*

tion, and the logic of deterrence will prevent the evolution of a world empire. The large powers will not be sufficiently cohesive and purposeful to impose their hegemony in the form of a concert and the small powers—while more energetically independent than in the past system—will still lack the unity of purpose to dominate. It is conceivable, however, that the nuclear powers might establish a "condominium" whereby they jointly guarantee the safety of non-nuclear powers, such as in the framework of a nonproliferation treaty. Nor can we count on a UN with a capacity for independent military action strikingly greater than is now incorporated in the familiar structure on the East River.

Totalitarian polities in Europe will become more benignly authoritarian as the process of bureaucratic *embourgeoisement* catapults them along the trajectory of the postindustrial society. The Western democracies will move further along the road they have taken, implying more internal division and less willingness to take energetic international action. In Latin America, a few countries will become left-wing totalitarian polities, nine or ten will succeed in modernizing as democracies, and the remainder will oscillate between degrees of authoritarianism, including many of the features we associate with the fascism of the 1930's. In Africa, the bulk of the nations will alternate between mild authoritarian and rigid totalitarian forms of government and national purpose, thus keeping alive ideological tensions on that continent after the demise of the present leadership. In Asia, things will be somewhat more stable, with an East and Southeast Asian radical communist bloc, a few successful democracies, and a large number of authoritarian polities trying to modernize in the more leisurely fashion of contemporary Pakistan. Under no conceivable circumstances can we count on more than fifty-odd democracies in a 133-member United Nations, but there may be as many as eighty authoritarian polities.

If the present ideological cleavages will not survive, how can these nations be grouped? The slight proliferation of nuclear weapons, the rise of a cohesive West Europe, and the arrival of a powerful Japan, first of all, will prevent the polarization of power we now associate with the United States' and the Soviet Union's leadership. Poles of power will give way to a more decentralized system of blocs lacking clear leaders. These blocs, moreover, will be organized functionally rather than geographically: economic objectives will dictate one kind of grouping for a country, military objectives will dictate another.

Thus we can imagine common markets functioning in West Europe, Latin America, and Central America, a self-contained communist trading system in Asia, an independent African bloc and one tied to Western Europe, and some kind of Asian "socialist" trading system for the noncommunist nations. In global terms, the Asian, African, and Latin-American economic blocs will be the "developing nations group" in UNCTAD and UNIDO, while West Europe, communist East Europe, Japan and the United States–Canadian complex will constitute their negotiating partner. In terms of national and bloc objectives, of course, the underdeveloped appear as the challengers of the international economic *status quo,* and the developed as its defenders. If there is to be an international class struggle, it will follow the lines of cleavage here suggested.

Military objectives, however, dictate a different pattern of bloc formation. It is probable that some form of attenuated East European bloc will linger on as understandings between the United States and Germany continue, while NATO decays. West Europe will be a weak military bloc, therefore, with some of its members seeking unity in nonalignment and others continuing to look to the United States. The United States and the Soviet Union, however, will be more on their own than at any time since 1948. All these formations will in essence be defenders of the *status quo*, territorially and militarily. In the Third World, none of the conceivable groupings will possess the power, cohesion, unity of purpose, or strong central institutions required to challenge any of the industrial blocs. In Africa there may emerge a bloc of totalitarian states bent on intervention and subversion and a defensive bloc of authoritarian ones anxious to fend off such challenges: but these two are unlikely to be coterminous with the economic blocs sketched above. In the Western Hemisphere, the familiar pattern of the OAS is likely to change soon, as the nations of the hemisphere split into Washington-oriented, Havana-inspired, and nonaligned blocs. The pro-American as well as the neutralist blocs will contain both democratic and authoritarian polities. In Asia, much depends on the future vigor of China. If Maoism remains forceful we may imagine a defensive military grouping of authoritarian and democratic nations (India, Indonesia, Malaysia, Iran, Thailand, Philippines, and perhaps Pakistan), an offensive grouping of China, North Korea, and Vietnam, and a bloc of genuine neutrals, such as Burma, Nepal, and Cambodia. If China were to become preoccupied with other matters, no military-ideological blocs need arise at all. In the UN, therefore, we would have a minimum of six or a maximum of ten military groupings, of varying cohesion and vastly different strengths, playing roles different from the economic blocs and offering a heterogeneous bundle of aspirations and demands as compared to past historical systems.

This very heterogeneity of blocs and objectives results in an untidy and confusing international distribution of power, which we label "asymmetric" because it lacks the more congruent, interfunctional bargaining characteristics of the current multipolar system. In that system, region, ideology, alliances, and modernity tend to covary. Nations will continue to use familiar means for attaining their objectives. But technology will give us more sophisticated devices than we now have for warfare, riot control, mind manipulation, technical assistance for economic development, mass education, and propaganda. Whether these imply a qualitative change in the nature of the system may well be doubted if we assume roughly equal access by all nations and blocs to the artifacts and techniques involved. The developing world will demand more aid of all kinds and more access to the markets of the developed. The industrial world will furnish more and more aid but also insist on spelling out conditions and limits. These transactions will go forward through bilateral as well as multilateral channels. As the West and the Soviet bloc tone down their respective propaganda campaigns, no such restraint will be observed between the West and the Third World and among the various blocs of developing nations. The entire range of social and human rights policy will be infected with these concerns and charges. Argument will continue over the conditions governing private foreign investment. More acrimony will be heard over the most "egalitarian redistributive" way of applying new knowledge to economic and social development; solutions may well confirm a decentralized and asymmetric pattern of accommodation, eliminating both superpowers as the sole font of action and ultimate authority. And, it almost goes without saying, the agitation for the complete elimination of all kinds of colonial rule will continue, as will sporadic warfare designed to hasten the process or defend against it.

This view of the future international system assumes further that the absolute military potency of the two superpowers will decline as the balance of nuclear terror continues between them, buttressed perhaps by additional but equal power in ABM systems and multiple warhead missiles. But nuclear proliferation would also continue, despite the existence of the nonproliferation treaty. Perhaps as many as twenty countries would acquire the capacity to produce hydrogen weapons; but only six or seven would also have the incentive and political motivation actually to do so. To the extent that such weapons are available to countries other than the five nations now brandishing them, the logic of mutual deterrence would apply in their relations with each other and the superpowers. The over-all military situation will remain untidy and unstructured, however, because of the unpredictable security aspirations of non-nuclear nations. If the now familiar congruence of economic, military, and ideological blocs is certain to fall apart, it will be replaced by a multilayered international system fragmented by separate national objectives.

Will these objectives, alignment patterns, and methods imply more enmeshment—or less—in multilateral processes? Economic development, decolonization, world trade, the status of human rights, and the diffusion of scientific and technological knowledge will almost certainly involve continuous international negotiation, even culminating in confrontation—whether verbal or financial. The nature of the evolving human environment leaves little room to expect anything less. The exception to this projection is the preservation of peace itself: the different character of the blocs and the asymmetric confrontation pattern between demands and means suggests that the bargaining pattern between collective security and decolonization or economic development objectives is a thing of the past. To have UN peacekeeping we must have an independent commitment of member nations, who accept it is good and desirable, not expediential, dependent on pay-offs in other issue areas. Such a commitment is unlikely to exist in the multibloc system.

And this has immediate implications for the tasks the UN will be expected to carry out. The members will insist on using the organization for the completion of decolonization, for energetic industrialization policies, for social modernization, for the regulation of world trade and finance, and even for propaganda broadsides in the field of human rights. It will almost certainly be used increasingly for social and economic planning and for the diffusion—controlled or not—of new knowledge. The point is, however, that each of these activities will be legitimate in its *own* right, with positive expectations attaching to *each* and little dependence on other issues or tasks. Therefore, the preservation of peace and the facilitation of peaceful change among the nations, *unless it also becomes an autonomous and legitimate task,* will not become legitimate by association with nonmilitary activities. There is nothing in the nature of a multibloc asymmetric system that gives us the right to expect such a development. As the tasks of the UN become legitimate, they also become self-encapsulating and self-sufficient, preventing the more precariously established tasks to profit from the success of the legitimate ones.

The choice for America is probably to seek national security through unilateral means, instead of relying on alliances or on UN peacekeeping; but there is no reason not to use peacekeeping operations for the limited and localized purposes that have proved successful. We ought to aid in the redistribution of the world's wealth if we believe in minimal standards of welfare even at the expense of slower domestic economic growth; toward this end we should welcome the continued enmeshment in UN and regional agencies, just as we should oppose it in the field of military security. We shall grow more dependent on world trade, as will everybody else; and we should draw the inference from this trend that more centralized world trade and monetary rules are desirable. This, however, implies nothing in the field of human rights, where we should reform our own society as we have been doing, without taking notice of the sniping of other nations and without seeking to tell them how to reform theirs. Hence with the atrophy of the UN's decolonization task, we should welcome the decline of the human rights task as well. And if we wish to reap the benefits of benign science as we discriminately apply new technology, we must make our peace with a true UN planning function much more enmeshing than the faltering steps taken so far. All this demands resistance to the course of automatic enmeshment. It demands thought, questioning, and even trepidation. It calls for the will and the desire to resist and remake an international system that grew as the unwilled result of earlier error.

United Nations Agencies

ECLA	Economic Commission for Latin America
ECOSOC	Economic and Social Council
EPTA	Expanded Program of Technical Assistance
FAO	Food and Agriculture Organization
IAEA	International Atomic Energy Administration
IBRD	International Bank for Reconstruction and Development
ICAO	International Civil Aviation Organization
IDA	International Development Association
IFC	International Finance Corporation
ILO	International Labor Organization
IMF	International Monetary Fund
ITO	International Trade Organization (never established)
ITU	International Telecommunications Union
SUNFED	Special UN Fund for Economic Development (never established)
UNCAST	UN Conference on the Application of Science and Technology to Developing Areas
UNCTAD	UN Conference on Trade and Development
UNDP	UN Development Program (formerly Special Fund and EPTA)
UNESCO	UN Educational, Scientific and Cultural Organization
UNIDO	UN Industrial Development Organization
UNITAR	UN Institute for Training and Research
UNRRA	UN Relief and Rehabilitation Administration (defunct)
WHO	World Health Organization
WMO	World Meteorological Organization

Other International Agencies

CENTO	Central Treaty Organization
CIAP	Inter-American Committee for the Alliance for Progress
COMECON	Council for Mutual Economic Assistance (East European)
EEC	European Economic Community
EFTA	European Free Trade Association
ENDC	Eighteen-Nation Disarmament Conference
EURATOM	European Atomic Energy Community
GATT	General Agreement on Tariffs and Trade
IA-ECOSOC	Inter-American Economic and Social Council (of the OAS)
IDB	Inter-American Development Bank
LAFTA	Latin American Free Trade Association
NATO	North Atlantic Treaty Organization
OAS	Organization of American States
OECD	Organization for Economic Cooperation and Development
OEEC	Organization for European Economic Cooperation (defunct)
SEATO	Southeast Asian Treaty Organization